GULBARGA · BIDAR · BIJAPUR

GULBARGA · BIDAR · BIJAPUR

Helen Philon

Photography by Clare Arni

JAICO PUBLISHING HOUSE

Ahmedabad Bangalore Bhopal Bhubaneswar Chennai
Delhi Hyderabad Kolkata Lucknow Mumbai

DECCAN HERITAGE
FOUNDATION

CONTENTS

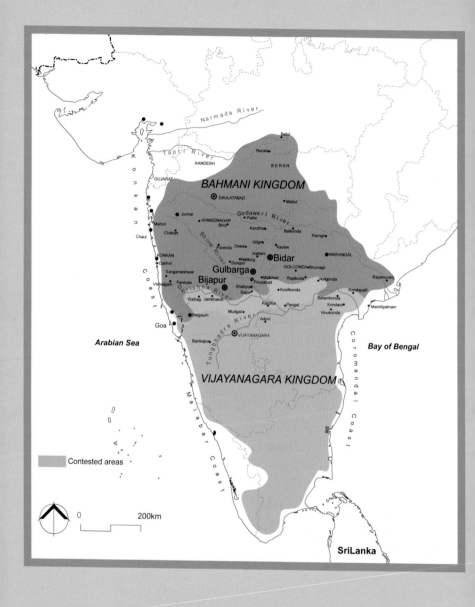

Gulbarga, Bidar and Bijapur in northern Karnataka are relatively unfamiliar destinations for visitors, both Indian and foreign. Yet these cities were once wealthy capitals of kingdoms in the Deccan, encompassing substantial parts of modern day Karnataka, Maharashtra, Andhra Pradesh and Goa. The Bahmani sultans of Gulbarga and Bidar in the 14th and 15th centuries controlled the entire region, from the Arabian Sea to the Bay of Bengal, south to the Vijayanagara kingdom. The Baridis controlled only the city of Bidar and a small area around it. In 1619, their territories became part of the Adil Shahi kingdom, which encompassed a much smaller domain than that of the Bahmanis. The Adil Shahi sultans ruled from Bijapur during the 16th and 17th centuries. While the Bahmani and Adil Shahi kingdoms have long vanished, the splendour of their courts at Gulbarga, Bidar and Bijapur may still be appreciated from the surviving monuments. Visitors are encouraged to travel to these historical centres, but upon arrival they will find a scarcity of reliable information. Hence the present volume, which aims to fill this gap by describing the principal buildings in and around these cities. If the visitors' time here awakens even a rudimentary interest in the history, architecture and art of the Bahmanis and Adil Shahis, then the author will be well satisfied.

In order to facilitate the visit to Gulbarga, Bidar and Bijapur, the guidebook is divided into separate chapters, each with a number of itineraries. The tour of Gulbarga starts with the fort in the middle of the city and then proceeds in a clockwise direction around the four quadrants of the surrounding urban core. For Bidar, the walled city is described first, followed by the fort, and then the surrounding monuments, beginning with the necropolis at Ashtur to the northeast. The Bijapur tour commences with the citadel in the middle, and then proceeds clockwise through the four quadrants of the city, before describing the outlying suburbs.

Map of the
Bahmani kingdom,
1347–c. 1500

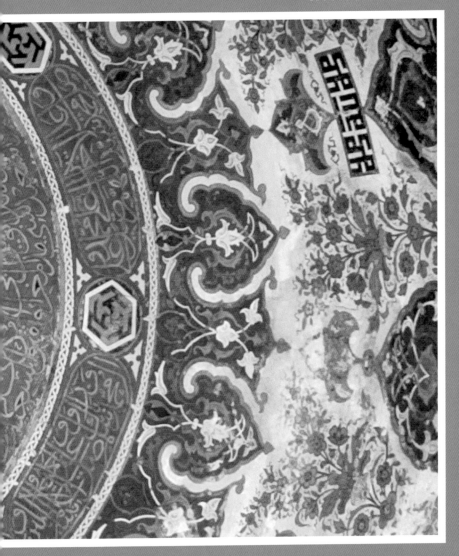

THE DECCAN REGION

PRECEDING PAGES:
Detail of the design
in the centre of
dome in the tomb
of Ahmad Shah
Wali, Ashtur,
Bidar, 1436

Bidar, Bijapur and Gulbarga are located in the middle of peninsular India, in the heart of a plateau known as the Deccan. (Deccan is an anglicised form of *dakkhin*, a term derived from the Sanskrit word *dakshina*, meaning south.) The Deccan begins to the south of the Gangetic plains of Northern India, from which it is separated by the Satpura and Vindhya ranges. The plateau rises to more than 1,000 metres at its southernmost point, where it is drained by the Kaveri river, known as the "Ganga of the South". Its eastern and western boundaries are defined by the Eastern and Western Ghats. From the Western Ghats rise the Narmada and the Tapti rivers, which run westwards to the Arabian Sea, while the Godavari and Krishna rivers flow eastwards from the Western Ghats to the Bay of Bengal, as do the Tungabhadra and Bhima after they merge with the Krishna.

The Deccan relies for its agricultural wealth on the monsoons and its age-old irrigation systems. The plains around Bidar are watered by the Manjira river, which joins the Godavari further east. Bidar's thick and porous laterite soil holds water well, which

View of the Manjira
river, Nimatabad,
Bidar

explains the abundance of wells, *baolis*, or step-wells, and reservoirs around the city. These are supplemented by *qanats*, or horizontal wells consisting of tunnels carved into the aquifer of the laterite plateau. This hydraulic system was invented in Iran, and introduced into the Deccan during the late 15th century by Iranian immigrants. *Qanats* comprise a line of wells with regularly spaced ventilation shafts with holes for drawing water. Another innovation of this period was the Persian Wheel, through which water is lifted in buckets attached to a wheel operated by animals circumambulating a platform. The abundance of water in combination with its fertile black soil contributed to Bidar's agricultural wealth, as did its strategic location with regard to its eastern provinces, which were rich in minerals and precious stones, including diamonds. Bidar was also conveniently situated for access to the Bay of Bengal ports, with their ocean-borne commercial relations. The city was therefore able to become a great commercial hub for the 15th-century trans-peninsular trade between the Arabian Sea and the Bay of Bengal.

Hydraulic device in Kumatgi: the corbels above the high wall support mechanisms that lift water to a series of elevated small tanks, Bijapur, 17th century

The cities of Gulbarga and Bijapur are located in basaltic lands with dominant black soil, rich in agricultural crops such as sugarcane, sunflower, gram and *bajra* (a type of millet). Several rivers traverse the plains of Gulbarga and must have contributed to its waterborne wealth, which helps explain why in 1350 Alauddin Bahman Shah, the first Bahmani sultan, chose this city for the capital of his newly founded kingdom. Gulbarga was surrounded by reservoirs that contributed to a rich verdant environment controlled by the ruler, a perfect location for the capital of the first Islamic Deccan kingdom.

Bijapur's 16th- and 17th-century irrigation systems are more varied than those of Gulbarga or Bidar. These comprised *qanats* and aqueducts, which permitted distant water resources to be accessed and conducted to the city, as well as *baolis* and reservoirs. In addition, local architects invented a novel hydraulic device, remains of which are seen at the palace resort of Kumatgi on the outskirts of Bijapur, that seems to have been adapted according to the Archimedes Principle. The Kumatgi water device employed corbels atop a high wall beside a well or reservoir to support mechanisms that lifted water to a series of elevated small tanks. Earthen pipes bedded in lime mortar connected these tanks to outlets at a lower level, the water being forced under high pressure.

RELIGIOUS, CULTURAL AND HISTORICAL BACKGROUND

Gulbarga, Bidar and Bijapur all lie in present-day northern Karnataka, an intermediary zone between two distinct linguistic zones: Marathi, which is part of the Indo-European family of languages, and Kannada, which belongs to the Dravidian group of languages. Before the arrival of the Delhi sultans at the end of the 13th century both these zones experienced the rise of popular,

devotional Bhakti movements. These were supported by the elite of the most important reigning kingdoms of the Deccan at the time: notably, the Yadavas of Devagiri, the Hoysalas of Dorasamudra, and the Kakatiyas of Warangal, in the northern, southern and eastern parts of the Deccan respectively. The texts relating to these movements express an egalitarian philosophy, wherein birth or status was not paramount in the performance of worship. Moreover, the use of vernacular languages rather than Sanskrit defined a new cultural milieu with a regional identity.

View of the Tungabhadra river, Vijayanagara

Among Marathi speakers in Maharashtra, the cult of Vithoba, a form of Vishnu, became the most important Bhakti movement; among Kannada speakers in Karnataka, the Lingayat movement prevailed, with its greatest apologist Basavan (died *c.* 1169), who rejected polytheism and the caste system, together with Brahmin supremacy. Here, the interaction between Lingayats and Sufis is evident at the *urs*, or annual death anniversary, of Ahmad Shah Wali at Ashtur on the outskirts of Bidar, at which the officiating head of the Lingayats performs the main rituals.

The Muslim conquests of the Deccan must be seen against this religious background. The presence of these Bhakti sects no doubt contributed to the socio-religious tensions which the invading Muslim armies turned to their advantage, explaining perhaps their rapid military success. After a number of invasions, commencing in 1296, the Deccan became a rich province of the Delhi sultanate under Muhammad Tughluq. The former headquarters of the Yadavas, Devagiri, renamed Daulatabad,

Queens' bath,
Vijayanagara,
c. 1500

became co-capital to Delhi in 1327. The power vacuum that followed Muhammad Tughluq's return to Delhi in 1334 prompted the local governors to declare independence, resulting in the simultaneous birth of two great Deccani powers: the Hindu kingdom of Vijayanagara, founded in 1336 at Hampi; and the Muslim Bahmani kingdom, founded in 1345, with successive capitals at Daulatabad (1347–50), Gulbarga (1350–1430) and Bidar (1430–c. 1520).

Constant warfare between Vijayanagara and the Bahmanis over the mineral-rich Raichur Doab, the well watered territory that lay between the Bhima and Tungabhadra rivers, did not discourage trade between these two kingdoms. Throughout more than 200 years of coexistence, there were numerous exchanges of artistic traditions and construction techniques. This resulted in a unique Deccani architectural vocabulary, which was further augmented by building forms and decorative motifs introduced from Arabia and

Dancing Turks,
Mahanavami
platform,
Vijayanagara,
14th century

Persia, as well as from Turkey and Central Asia. East African slaves, known as Habshis, were welcomed in the Deccan; indeed, from the 16th century onwards they came to occupy leading positions in the political life of the region.

This multi-ethnic environment enriched the cultures of the Deccan, but was also responsible for socio-political and religious tensions. The Habshis, local Islamic communities and Muslims who had migrated to the Deccan from Northern India during the early invasions belonged to a powerful group known as Dakhinis, while immigrants from the Arab-, Iranian- and Turkish-speaking lands were known as Afaqis, foreigners, or *gharbian*, Westerners. The power struggle between these two groups ultimately contributed to the fall of the Bahmani kingdom in the early 16th century and the rise of a number of successor dynasties, of which only two concern us here: the Adil Shahis of Bijapur and the Baridis of Bidar. Strife between Dakhinis and Afaqis continued during the rule of these successor dynasties into the 16th and 17th centuries, to the advantage of the Mughals of Northern India who intruded into the Deccan from the end of the 16th century onwards. By 1686, Sikandar Adil Shah of Bijapur had capitulated to the Mughals, and the city together with its territories became part of the Mughal Deccan province. In the course of the 18th century, Bijapur, Gulbarga and Bidar were absorbed into Asaf Jahi state, which had its capital at Hyderabad (1724–1950). In 1760, Bijapur was annexed by the Marathas after the defeat of the Asaf Jahis, and passed to the princely state of Satara in 1818. In 1848, Bijapur merged with the Bombay Presidency.

While Bahmani rulers officially sponsored Sunni Islam, they privately patronised Sufi figures, such as Sheikh Sirajuddin Junaidi, whose *dargah*, or funerary complex, in Gulbarga still attracts devotees. Firuz Shah Bahmani (r. 1398–1422) did not sponsor any particular *dargah*, but his inquiring mind alerted him to different mystical traditions, without however dissociating the Bahmani throne from the *dargah* of Sheikh Sirajuddin Junaidi that had been sponsored by his predecessors. Ahmad Shah, Firuz Shah's brother and successor (r. 1422–36), was a follower of the Chishti Gesu Daraz and patronised his *dargah* during his short reign in Gulbarga. After relocating the Bahmani capital to Bidar in 1432, Ahmad Shah switched allegiance, inviting Shah Nimatullah, a great Iranian Sufi, to settle in Bidar and become his spiritual preceptor. In the following years Shah Nimatullah's descendants intermarried with the royal family, remaining as spiritual advisors to the Bahmanis, though losing importance under later Deccani rulers.

The Baridi successors to the Bahmanis were Sunnis, while the Adil Shahis of Bijapur vacillated between Sunnism and Shi'ism. Adherents of several Sufi sects settled in Bijapur in the 16th and 17th centuries. Aside from the Chishti order, which remained the most prominent sect in the Deccan, the Qadiris also gained importance, as did, to a lesser degree, the Shattaris.

A number of Bahmani and Adil Shahi visionary rulers and leaders were responsible for shaping the political and cultural

The Adil Shahi Dynasty, c. 1680 Muhammad, Kamal; Muhammad, Chand © 2011, The Metropolitan Museum of Art/Art Resource/SCALA, Florence

The ruined palaces in the royal enclosure with the Bhima river in the background, Firuzabad, c. 1400

environment of the wider Deccan. Sultan Firuz Shah was multilingual and is supposed to have been able to converse with his many wives from different regions in their native tongues. Educated in religious and literary matters, he continued and strengthened the open immigration policies started by his predecessors, organising expeditions to find the most gifted individuals and bring them to settle in the Deccan. Firuz Shah was thereby responsible for the introduction into the region of building types from Anatolia in present day Turkey, notably *hammams*, or baths, as well as buildings with cross-in-square layouts, and another type of building inspired by the ceremonial structures described in the *Shahnama*, the 10th-century Persian epic of Firdowsi, as well as in the poems of Saadi. Firuz Shah was the first Deccan sultan to marry the daughter of a Hindu raja; in this case, the ruler of Vijayanagara, thereby promoting a dialogue between imported and local traditions, and initiating the composite culture that was to typify the region. He was also the first Deccani ruler to encroach on orthodox Islam by blurring the distinction between Sufi and sultan. Ahmad Shah Bahmani, known also as Wali, or Friend of God, was considered the Khalifa, or designated successor, of the Nimatullahi sect, thereby underscoring the political and mystical roles of kingship. These roles were further promoted by Ibrahim II, the Adil Shahi sultan of Bijapur, during the 17th century. Ahmad Shah Bahmani, however, remains the only sultan in the Deccan to be venerated both by Muslims and Hindus, as evidenced to this day during his *urs* at Ashtur.

The most powerful personality of the Bahmani kingdom in the second half of the 15th century was Mahmud Gawan, a noble immigrant merchant from Gilan in Iran. His wisdom, education and international contacts impressed the Bahmani rulers and helped him rise to the highest echelons of government. Mahmud Gawan reorganised the administration of the Bahmani state and attempted to resolve the ongoing dispute between the warring Afaqi and Dakhini factions, a policy which led tragically to his violent murder in 1482. Under Mahmud Gawan, new defensive structures were erected that contributed to the kingdom's strength, safeguarding it from enemy invasions. The magnificent, unique *madrasa* that he built in Bidar, which to this day bears his name, is a tribute to Mahmud Gawan's homeland, as well as a testimony to this figure's profound appreciation of his adopted land and kingdom.

Detail from the *madrasa* of Mahmud Gawan, Bidar, 1472

While the later Baridi sultans of Bidar have left some exceptional monuments, contemporary documents describe an ambitious, belligerent group of rulers eager to control the riches that they inherited from the Bahmanis. In contrast, the Adil Shahis were, for the most part, refined and educated figures, eager to make their kingdom a stronghold of glorious Deccani culture. History singles out Ali I Adil Shah of Bijapur, who belonged to the confederacy of sultans responsible for destroying the kingdom of Vijayanagara and acquiring the much coveted Raichur Doab with its mineral riches. Together with his successors, Ibrahim II and Muhammad Adil Shah, Ali I is believed to epitomise the Deccani spirit of openness and cultural refinement that was first aspired to by the Bahmanis.

URBAN TYPOLOGIES

Gulbarga, Bijapur and Bidar are all associated with Bahmani rule, as is the royal city of Firuzabad founded by Firuz Shah in about 1399. From c. 1500 until 1616, Bidar became the capital of the small Baridi kingdom, but proudly retained the urban design of its predecessors. Bijapur, also the capital of a former Bahmani province, was developed by the Adil Shahi dynasty (c. 1500–1760), especially after the Battle of Talikota in 1565, becoming the most important western Deccani cultural centre and capital of a politically and economically influential kingdom.

In all three capitals, royal edifices were located within circular or elliptical forts, whose layouts harked back to previous Hindu traditions. In each case, however, different layouts were established for the urban core, where commercial, religious and other community institutions were located. Though Gulbarga was supplied with an elliptical fort, originally ringed with earthen ramparts, there is a notable absence of urban fortifications, probably because the city was dominated by the ceremonial needs of its elite. The earliest part of Gulbarga was laid out in the vicinity of the *Jami Masjid*, or congregational mosque, (known in Gulbarga as the Shah Bazaar Mosque) directly to the north of Gulbarga Fort. From c. 1400, a new urban quarter grew up to the east of the fort, probably to service the pilgrims visiting the *dargah* of Gesu Daraz that was located in this direction.

The existence of secondary co-capitals and royal suburbs is typical of Deccani cities. Gulbarga boasted Firuzabad, 30 kilometres to the south. Here, the circular urban form was altogether abandoned in favour of an almost square plan, a layout that may have been introduced into the Deccan by immigrants from Iran, Anatolia or Central Asia. Immediately northwest of Gulbarga lies the royal suburb of Sultanpur, where a ruined palace and

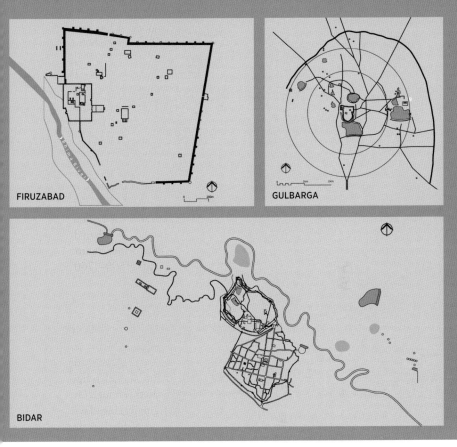

Plans of Bahmani cities

congregational mosque can still be seen. Bidar, the second capital of the Bahmanis and capital of the successor Baridi dynasty, combines a circular fort with a lozenge-shaped walled city. The Bahmanis in Bidar do not seem to have had any co-capitals, opting instead for two nearby royal suburbs: Nimatabad on the banks of the Manjira river, and Kamthana, northwest of Bidar Fort. Bijapur was laid out as an approximately circular walled city, with an additional circular walled citadel at its core. Bijapur had two royal foundations on the western and northwestern edge of the city, at Shahpur and at Nauraspur, the latter supplied with a ceremonial complex located in the middle of a unique, nine-sided walled enclosure. There were also several outlying suburbs, including Ainapur and Kumatgi beyond the eastern walls of the city. (see map, inside back cover)

TOMBS

The most characteristic building type of Deccani sultanate architecture is the tomb, which is found standing alone or as part of a royal or Sufi funerary complex. Tombs were usually set on raised platforms, situated in arable lands or surrounded by gardens, and were always located near a water source. Bahmani tombs of the 14th century are indebted to Northern Indian Tughluq practice. They are square in plan with sloping walls topped by merlons and a crowning hemispherical dome. From the end of the 14th century, tomb walls become vertical and their domes more pronounced, while the merlons and rooftop corner pinnacles display more elaborate designs. From about the second quarter of the 15th century, tomb structures grow in size, reaching monumental proportions by the middle of the 17th century, as evidenced in the two royal necropolises at Bidar and the royal tombs of Bijapur. None of the royal Bahmani funerary monuments are inscribed, and we cannot be certain to whom they belonged; their present attributions are based solely on tradition. In contrast, some of the Baridi and Adil Shahi mausolea are inscribed and dated.

Several Baridi and Adil Shahi tombs abandon the enclosed square building type in preference for an airy arrangement, wherein the burial chamber has arched openings on four sides or, as in some cases in Bijapur, is surrounded by an arcaded verandah. Royal sepulchres in both Gulbarga and Bidar adjoin water bodies, or are spatially coordinated with the tomb of their Sufi teacher along an east-west axis. One striking Bahmani feature is the absence of an accompanying mosque or *idgah*, an open-air prayer platform (with the exception of the tomb of Alauddin Hasan Bahman Shah in Gulbarga), a situation that was to change under the Baridis and the Adil Shahis. Baridi royal mausolea to the west of Bidar are set within enclosed orthogonal landscaped gardens in which a mosque and hostels for visiting pilgrims and/or family members were combined with irrigation works located

Example of an early Bahmani tomb, Gulbarga, c. 1400

outside the walls. Adil Shahi royal tombs are spread around the city and suburbs of Bijapur, and many are associated with a mosque. In Bahmani Sufi *dargahs*, the tomb of the saint was always associated with the *jama'at khana*, or pilgrims' hostel, which could also serve as accommodation for the saint's *murids*, or disciples.

MOSQUES AND *IDGAHS*

Three types of mosques are found at Gulbarga, Bidar and Bijapur. The congregational mosques, or first type, consist of multiple-bay domed units within a walled courtyard, entered through a domed gateway on axis with the main *mihrab*, or prayer niche, of the prayer hall. This *mihrab* always projects on the exterior of the *qibla* wall, as is true of all mosques. Some congregational mosques have a special enclosure for the ruler, usually located in the northwestern section

Plan of the Shah Bazaar Jami, Gulbarga

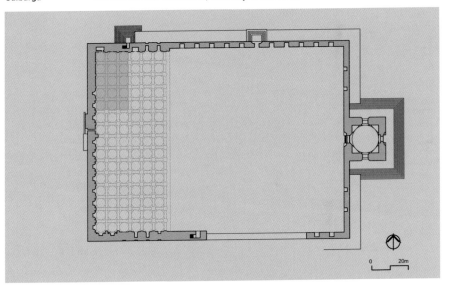

0   20m

of the prayer hall (for example, the Shah Bazaar Mosque in Gulbarga and the *Jami Masjid* in Firuzabad). The second type, to which belong the majority of mosques, shares the same configuration, but lacks any courtyard or domed entrance gate. Of an entirely different layout, and lacking these features, are a few mosques consisting of a vaulted prayer hall with transverse arches running parallel to their main façade. This third type includes the Langarki mosque in Gulbarga and the mosque of Ali Shahid Pir in Bijapur. Differing from Bahmani congregational mosques, the *Jami Masjid* of Bijapur is unfinished, but had a gate framed by stone corridors on its northern side; the entrance on the east is an addition of the Mughal period. A number of Bijapur's mosques had multi-storeyed gated entrances. The most celebrated of these is the Mihtar Mahal, with its novel construction and decorative details. The parapets of all Deccani mosques were decorated with merlons and corner *guldastas*, or pinnacles. These motifs were greatly enriched at Bijapur, where a playful use of multiple pinnacles is combined with polygonal minarets and *chhatris*, or open rooftop pavilions.

Idgahs have a raised platform on the west side of which is the *qibla* wall with *mihrabs*, the central *mihrab* protruding on its exterior. Next to the central *mihrab* is a stone *minbar*, or pulpit, that could also have functioned as the ruler's throne, as is evident from the *idgah* adjoining the Chor Gumbad in Gulbarga.

PALACES

Royal residences of the Bahmani, Baridi and Adil Shahi sultans were usually located in the fortified enclosures of the capitals, as well as in the secondary capitals or royal suburbs. These palaces probably fulfilled the different ceremonial needs of the respective courts.

Two types of Deccani ceremonial halls are found in the 14th and early-15th centuries. *Iwan*-like audience halls with a north-south orientation were distinguished by two-storeyed

Iwan, an arched vaulted audience hall, open on one side, Firuzabad, c. 1400

Dargah of Khalifat Al-Rahman, outside the walled city of Firuzabad, *c.* 1400

vaulted spaces with transverse arches that continued the Northern Indian architectural traditions imported into the Deccan by the Tughluqs. Such structures are evident in Firuzabad and at the Bala Hisar in Gulbarga Fort (the latter engulfed by later Adil Shahi period masonry). The second type of ceremonial hall combines a multi-columned space with a domed square space. The example in Gulbarga Fort, datable to 1407, is a physical interpretation of the royal and spiritual concepts of power that were disseminated throughout the Islamic world thanks to the *Shahnama*, (mentioned above). Neither the *iwan*-like audience hall nor the multi-columned hall, known in the *Shahnama* as a *hazar sutun* and seen in Gulbarga, survived the move to Bidar, where a new set of architectural power symbols emerged.

The layouts of the informal private palaces of the Bahmanis were adopted for the country villas of the sultans and provincial governors. Built of stone and timber with tripartite façades, these structures each comprised a columned hall flanked by lesser rooms. Around 1440, this palace type was revived by Alauddin Bahman Shah in Bidar, but on a monumental scale, and was then repeated in various configurations in the numerous audience halls of the Adil Shahis. The royal associations of these tripartite buildings are indicated by domes and by two new features: the presence of water and the axial change of level. In the ceremonial palaces of the Adil Shahis, the dome was replaced by a majestic arch, which was often reflected in a pool located in front. Beneath the apex of this arch was a royal loggia sheltered by a small dome on pendentives, while the entire façade followed a tripartite scheme.

Two additional types of royal structures were developed at Firuzabad: the cross-in-square building, first attested at the *dargah* of Khalifat al-Rahman outside the walled city, which we believe originally functioned as a royal audience hall; and the *hammam*, of which at least two examples survive within the city itself. Both these architectural types were probably introduced to the Deccan by immigrants from Anatolia in present-day Turkey.

Eastern gateway, Firuzabad, *c.* 1400

Gatehouses also have royal associations, as it was here that taxes were levied and the flow of people and goods controlled. Gates were often two-storeyed, with platforms for guards on either side of a passage. But they might also be domed, indicating a ceremonial purpose, as is the southern gate in Gulbarga Fort and the Gumbad Darwaza in Bidar.

BUILDING MATERIALS

Basalt was the primary building material in Gulbarga and Bijapur, laterite in Bidar, with occasional use of harder and more expensive granite; brick was preferred for domes or vaults owing to its comparative lightness. Basalt bedded in mortar gave tremendous solidity to structures, such as the ceiling in the burial chamber at the Ibrahim Rauza in Bijapur. This mostly flat ceiling is composed of massive slabs of dolerite, a fine-to-medium greenish basalt, which were bonded by the excellent mortar developed by the Adil Shahi builders. Equally high-quality mortar was used to secure the rubble stonework of the colossal dome of the Gol Gumbad in Bijapur.

The Indian vision of an ideal world is that of a blooming, flourishing, lush and verdant landscape. For this reason, gardens are found throughout the Deccan, not only in the royal enclosures in the middle of Bijapur, but also in suburban resorts such as Kumatgi, Shahpur and Nauraspur, as well as in the royal enclosures and necropolises at Bidar, Gulbarga and Holkonda. Gardens probably once existed within all these cities, as in the case of the deer park near the Taj Baoli in Bijapur, thus contributing to a lush urban realm. Such congenial environments are now sadly replaced by the grey, dark and austere scorched scenery that greets visitors today.

ARCHITECTURAL DECORATION

Wood carved ceiling, Rangini Mahal, Bidar Fort, c. 1500

The various decorative techniques and themes that embellish the monuments at Gulbarga, Bidar and Bijapur were shared by both secular and religious structures. The exception is the depiction

of human figures and animals, which, apart from the southern wall in the tomb of Firuz Shah at Gulbarga, is found only on ceremonial structures and pleasure pavilions. Decorative themes typically comprise foliate designs of spirals, lotuses, banana buds and other vegetation, together with geometric motifs and inscriptions. The most prominent decorative techniques were plasterwork, stone carving and wood carving. The flammable quality of wood explains its scarcity, although the rare examples that survive, most notably in the Rangini Mahal in Bidar Fort, indicate a remarkable artistic virtuosity. Other decorative techniques included ceramic revetments and painting.

In mosques, tombs and palaces, the favoured decorative medium was painted

Detail of carved basalt columns, Palace II (Takht Mahal), Bidar Fort, c. 1440

plasterwork, on which foliate and geometrical themes were applied together with inscriptions. By the 15th century, the adoption of dark-grey basalt and deep-green dolerite for columns, pilasters, column bases, *chhajjas*, or stone awnings, and door frames added

Basalt doorway,
inlaid with mother
of pearl, Rangini
Mahal, Bidar Fort,
c. 1543–80

Carved stucco designs, Rangini Mahal, Bidar Fort, c. 1500

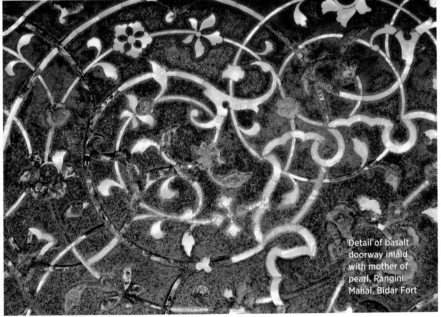

Detail of basalt doorway inlaid with mother of pearl, Rangini Mahal, Bidar Fort

Carved stucco design on the tomb of Shah Rukh Khan, Ashtur, Bidar, c. 1500

Column and ceiling in carved timber at the *mandapa* in Rangini Mahal, Bidar Fort, c. 1500

chromatic effects to the exterior surfaces. To the same traditions are credited the beautifully-carved timber columns, ceilings and pyramidal vaults. This combination of plasterwork, stone carving and timberwork continued throughout the 15th and 16th centuries, together with new ceramic techniques, notably the brilliantly coloured, underglaze tiles and glazed tile mosaics that were introduced from Central Asia. In addition to these techniques, we must also consider the textiles and carpets. Though nothing now survives of these from the Bahmani period, a few rare examples from the Adil Shahi era testify to their luxurious texture and appearance. There are a few instances of inlaid stonework, a laborious technique that became widespread during the Mughal period. An outstanding decorative feature unique to the Deccan was mother-of-pearl inlaid into polished basalt, as seen in the Rangini Mahal in Bidar Fort. This technique may have originated in the inlaid metallic designs that embellished the cannons of the period.

A few faint remains of mural paintings survive on the dome of the Gumbad Darwaza in Bidar, while the many black outlines of flowers on the walls of the Takht Mahal in Bidar suggest that painted designs were widely used in conjunction with tilework and engaged carved-basalt columns. The leafy forms and designs on the dome of the Gumbad Darwaza in Bidar recall the better-preserved murals in the tomb of Ahmad Shah Wali at Ashtur, suggesting that the same artists may have worked on both buildings. The varied designs on the tomb evince the cosmopolitan environment of Deccani courtly culture. They may be linked with the Central Asian Timurid school of painting, which introduced a visual language of power that came to be accepted by Muslim dynasties throughout the Middle East and India. Additional murals are also found in the Asar Mahal in Bijapur and the nearby royal resort of Kumatgi. The Kumatgi paintings are closely related to miniature paintings of the period, while those of the Asar Mahal

Murals in the tomb
of Ahmad Shah
Wali, Ashtur, Bidar,
1436

depict rotund, bejewelled ladies wearing transparent garments.
These murals may be the work of Deccani artists familiar with
contemporary European pictorial traditions.

GULBARGA

PRECEDING PAGES:
**Squinch of dome
in _Jami Masjid_,
Gulbarga Fort, 1407**

The earthen fort of Gulbarga became the residence of the
Bahmani sultans in 1350, when they shifted their capital here
from Daulatabad. By making this move, the Bahmanis showed they
were keen to establish an identity independent from that of their
predecessors, the Tughluqs, who had chosen Daulatabad as their
Deccani co-capital. It is also likely that the choice of this location
was dictated by its proximity to the mineral rich, well watered
Raichur Doab. This zone was to be constantly contested between
the Bahmanis and the rulers of Vijayanagara, their major rivals to
the south. After the Bahmanis'
demise at the beginning of the
16th century, Gulbarga passed
to their successors, the Baridis,
and from them to the Adil
Shahis who controlled the city
from 1619 onwards. By the end
of the 17th century, Gulbarga
had become part of the Mughal
Empire. By 1750, it was absorbed
into the Asaf Jahi territories.

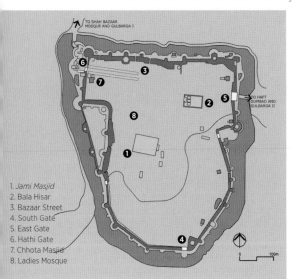

1. _Jami Masjid_
2. Bala Hisar
3. Bazaar Street
4. South Gate
5. East Gate
6. Hathi Gate
7. Chhota Masjid
8. Ladies Mosque

Gulbarga Fort

GULBARGA FORT

Some of the most important
ceremonial structures of the
Bahmani sultans are to be seen
inside Gulbarga Fort. They
comprise two audience halls,
one commonly known as the _Jami Masjid_, the royal bazaar, and
three gates.

The grey basalt fort walls that greet visitors today belong to
the 17th-century Adil Shahi period, when Gulbarga reverted to the
status of a frontier city. It was at this time that the metal foundries
of the city were established. These workshops were responsible
for some of the wrought-iron canons that still can be seen on the
bastions of the Fort and the great free-standing keep inside the
ramparts known as the Bala Hisar. It is also likely that the Adil
Shahi period saw the construction of the stone revetments and
circular bastions that encased earlier tapering earthen walls. In
Bahmani times, the only stone features of the Fort were the main

Enclosure walls and moat, Gulbarga Fort, 14th century and later

gates on the east, south and northwest, the last known as the Hathi Darwaza. Lesser stone gates were located along the inner curtain wall around the western section of the Fort.

This tour of Gulbarga Fort begins at the East Gate. Framed by circular bastions, the arched façade of this gate opens onto a rectangular passage with transverse arches. This leads into a corridor flanked by raised platforms with steps up to their roofs. In plan, this gate relates to those in Firuzabad (described below), suggesting dates during the reign of Firuz Shah Bahmani. From this structure, one could originally reach the eastern portion of the city, here termed Gulbarga II, and from there the reservoir that was either built or repaired by Firuz Shah, around which are disposed the *dargahs* of Gesu Daraz and Sheikh Mujarrad, as well as the royal necropolis of Haft Gumbad.

The interior of Gulbarga Fort is dominated by the imposing, windowless and buttressed Bala Hisar, directly opposite the East Gate. On climbing the steps leading to the top of this solid stronghold, visitors will encounter the remains of transverse arches. These must have once belonged to the two-storeyed, *iwan*-like

The stronghold of Bala Hisar, Gulbarga Fort, c. 1380 and later

audience hall of Muhammad I and his successors, dating from about 1358–1400. More steps give access to the roof, where a locally-manufactured cannon can be seen. Nearby is the *Jami Masjid* and Ladies' Mosque; to the west, beyond the Fort, may be glimpsed the monumental Chor Gumbad together with its surrounding *idgahs*.

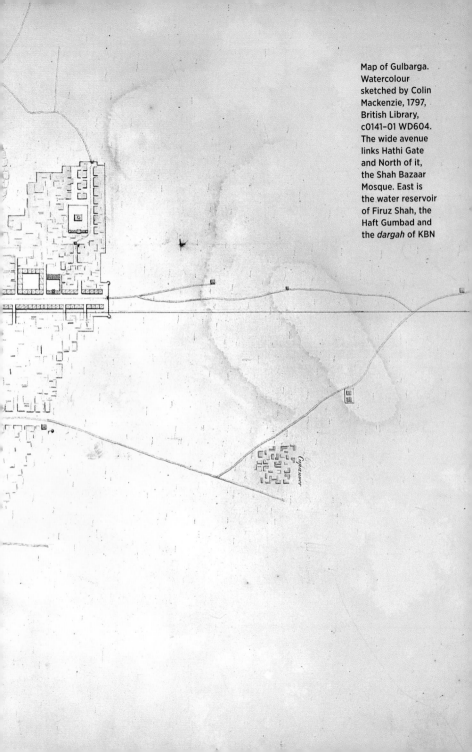

Map of Gulbarga. Watercolour sketched by Colin Mackenzie, 1797, British Library, c0141-01 WD604. The wide avenue links Hathi Gate and North of it, the Shah Bazaar Mosque. East is the water reservoir of Firuz Shah, the Haft Gumbad and the *dargah* of KBN

Captaeney

The so-called *Jami Masjid*, originally an audience hall, is
commonly known as a congregational mosque, and dated to the
early Bahmani period thanks to an inscription of 1367 discovered in
nearby debris in the early-20th century and then embedded into its
northern entrance portal. This unique building is remarkable for its
austere appearance and bold architectural forms. Wide side aisles
on three sides have broad transverse arches covered by vaults, while
the numerous square bays of the interior are roofed with domes
on corbelled pendentives. These architectural elements point to
a date in the early-15th century, and to a later remodelling when
the building was changed from audience hall to mosque, probably
sometime after 1700. The majestic main dome, with arches on
columns displayed on its drum, sits on trilobed arched squinches
and shelters a raised square platform where the building's only

mihrab is located. The baluster columns on this *mihrab* first appear in the Deccan under the Asaf Jahis in the 18th century, suggesting that this niche must be a post-Bahmani addition.

Several features challenge the identification of this building as a congregational mosque: its limited public accessibility, since it was located inside the royal enclosure of the fort; the absence of a protrusion marking the location of the *mihrab* on the exterior *qibla* wall; and the lack of a courtyard and domed square gatehouse on axis with the main *mihrab* of the prayer hall. The walled protrusion, courtyards and domed gatehouse are typical of Bahmani congregational mosques; their absence here suggests that this building was not originally intended as a mosque, even though its orientation on an east-west axis would have permitted it to be used as place of prayer.

South of the *Jami Masjid*, en route to the South Gate of the Fort, are two unidentified buildings and several *baolis*. The South Gate is buried under silting and sedimentation. Its internal façade, which is evident, comprises an arched opening to a square domed chamber, now buried, that must have given access to the reservoir outside the Fort on this side. Framing this arched façade are *mandapa*-like structures built with reused Chalukya period temple material.

Bazaar Street, now occupied by squatters, Gulbarga Fort, *c.* 1400

This tour passes by the Ladies' Mosque to the northwest of the *Jami Masjid*. This triple-domed-bay mosque with an overhanging *chhajja* has three *mihrabs*, between which are embedded reused temple columns and small arched niches. From the Ladies' Mosque visitors should proceed in a northerly direction so as to reach the 16th-century Chhota Masjid, with its large, deep pool. This multi-domed mosque is adorned with foliate motifs and inscriptions, mostly Quranic suras, invocations and blessings.

From the Chhota Masjid, visitors may cross to the fort's royal Bazaar Street, one of the best-preserved such thoroughfares in the Deccan, now occupied by squatters. The street comprises a long, wide avenue that commenced close to the Bala Hisar and ended at the inner portal of the Hathi Darwaza. The street is lined with parallel rows of square chambers sheltered by *chhajjas*, roofed with differently decorated pyramidal vaults.

At the end of the Bazaar Street, and probably serving as the principal entrance to Gulbarga Fort, is the Hathi Darwaza, the only truly defensive entrance to the fort. This gate is contiguous with the Bazaar Street inside the citadel, to which it was linked by another avenue with shops that led to the piazza in front of the only congregational mosque of the capital, the Shah Bazaar Mosque. These two commercial avenues contributed to the creation of the thoroughfares used by the Bahmani sultan when he exited the fort to attend the Friday prayers at the congregational mosque known in Gulbarga as the Shah Bazaar mosque.

The Hathi Darwaza's long, winding passageway is protected by massive outworks found in no other Bahmani gatehouse. The passageway begins at the courtyard on the northwestern side of the gateway, with its typical Bahmani raised platforms and reused temple columns. During the succeeding centuries (16th and 17th centuries), this layout evolved into an impressive defensive structure with five doors and three checkpoints. The passageway ends in two bastions facing the wide shopping avenue that leads to the Shah Bazaar Mosque. Along this winding passageway are different structures dating from the 15th century onwards.

From the Hathi Darwaza, visitors may continue westwards to inspect the tombs of the first Bahmani sultans and the Chor Gumbad; alternatively,they may follow the road that runs northwest from the Shah Bazaar mosque in order to reach the *dargah* of Sheikh Sirajuddin Junaidi with its impressive façade framed by two imposing minarets.

WEST OF THE FORT

Aligned with the *dargah* of Sheikh Junaidi to the west of Gulbarga Fort are the tombs of the first three Bahmani sultans: Alauddin Hasan Gangu, founder of the dynasty, who was crowned as Alauddin Shah Bahmani in 1347, dying 11 years later; Muhammad I (d. 1375); and Muhammad II (d. 1398). All three tombs are bold, unadorned edifices, the first two with tapering walls in the typical Tughluq tradition. The merlons and corner rooftop finials are features that recur in all later Bahmani tombs and mosques. Attached to the *qibla* wall of Alauddin Shah's tomb is an *idgah*, on which rests the cenotaph of Hasan Gangu's prime minister and friend, Saifuddin Ghori.

Nearby is the Kharbuja Gumbad (*c.* 1420). This small tomb has four arched openings topped by a lobed dome, indicating that it might have originally been a garden pavilion. Its whitewashed interior is filled with elaborate stucco designs that must have once

Chor Gumbad, Gulbarga, early 15th century

been painted, as is suggested by another mausoleum further north, Jacha bi Gumbad, or the tomb of Alauddin Hasan Gangu's seventh wife. This structure is open on three sides, and its interior filled with rubble from the now damaged cenotaphs. Its *mihrab* and dome, where remains of the original painted designs can still be seen, are beautifully decorated with Quranic inscriptions, lotus scrolls and leaf-shaped trees filled with lotus flowers in the shape of scrolls.

On a hill about a kilometre west of these tombs is the Chor Gumbad. This monumental domed structure contains no burials, indicating that it was never intended as a tomb, but may have been erected by Ahmad Shah to commemorate his victory over his brother, Firuz Shah, and his return to the throne in 1422, thanks to the support of his *pir*, or spiritual advisor, Gesu Daraz. The façades of the Chor Gumbad are divided into tiers of arched recesses, with an entrance on its eastern face. Its dome inside is decorated with a band of stucco scrolls, on which rest leaf-shaped tree motifs filled with scrolls. From the southern *iwan*, two sets of steps lead to an upper-level corridor that was originally screened by *jalis*, probably intended to accommodate the ladies of the Bahmani court. The stairs continue to the rooftop, where there is a quartet of *chhatris*, or open-pillared kiosks, decorated with lobed domes.

Detail of stucco ornament, with leaf-shaped tree motif filled with scrolls, on the inside of the dome of the Chor Gumbad

NORTH OF THE FORT

Gulbarga's original urban core most likely began at the courtyard fronting the westernmost entrance of the Hathi Darwaza. From this courtyard, a road lined with shops, as suggested by surviving architectural remains embedded in later structures, leads to the earliest part of the city, bypassing the Shah Bazaar Mosque, the only congregational mosque in Gulbarga which is located off this main avenue. This mosque, which was founded in the 14th century, with repairs dating from the time of Firuz Shah Bahmani (*c.* 1400), stands on a platform on the western side of a square where a lively vegetable market unfolds every morning. Visitors should ask one of the merchants to direct them to the person holding the key to the mosque.

Closely resembling the ruined mosque in Firuzabad (described below), the Shah Bazaar is rectangular in plan and is framed by stone walls that must have had two openings on each of the northern and southern sides. A monumental flight of steps on the east leads to the domed gate pavilion with its four doors, the northern and southern ones now blocked, which gives access into an unpaved courtyard lined with blind arched niches. Stairs attached to the courtyard wall on the southern side lead to the roof of the prayer hall. Fifteen aisles of six domed-bay units on corbelled pendentives run perpendicular to the *qibla* wall. At the end of each aisle is a *mihrab*, with the central *mihrab*, distinguished by four echoing arched panels. Beside this *mihrab* is a three-stepped *minbar*, and a door leading to a narrow passage abutting the *mihrab* projection on the exterior wall of the *qibla*, suggesting that this section of the mosque was once connected to another structure. Signs of timber construction above the floor level in the three aisles on the northeastern corner of the mosque mark the place of the *muluk khana*, or royal enclosure, with its three *mihrabs*.

Leaving the Shah Bazaar Mosque, visitors should walk along the broad, straight street running to the west. This terminates in the impressive ceremonial gateway of the *dargah* of Sheikh Sirajuddin Junaidi, who, until his death in 1380, was the spiritual advisor of the early Bahmani sultans. The arched double-storeyed symmetrical gateway, added in the 17th century during the Adil Shahi period, is framed by minarets with cylindrical shafts and balconies. The central domed passage that once led to the rather unimpressive *dargah* compound is now interrupted by an enclosure wall that has altered the original plan of the complex. Progressing southwards, visitors will encounter a broken temple column at the corner of this enclosure wall. Opposite the southwestern wall of the *dargah*, and on the north-south axis of the saint's tomb, is a dilapidated structure that may once have functioned as a pilgrims' hostel within the *dargah* compound. Just before reaching the gardens that surround the mosque and the tombs, visitors will encounter a step-well with a Persian inscription recording that it was built by Abu Muhammad Tabrizi in 1367.

Mausoleum and college of Sirajuddin near Gulbarga, March 1797. Watercolour sketched by C. Mackenzie, British Library, WD605

43

The recently repainted dome in the tomb of Sheikh Sirajuddin Junaidi, *c.* 1400 or 16th–17th century

Two tombs are inside the walled compound of the *dargah* of Sheikh Sirajuddin Junaidi. Above the main entrance of the tomb closest to the mosque is a Persian inscription dated 1380, declaring it as the mausoleum of the saint; the tomb nearby is that of the saint's son. Both tombs share the same interiors, being decorated with foliate designs and stucco inscriptions. Though these motifs relate to Bahmani examples, they could date from the Adil Shahi period; they have been recently repainted in gaudy colours. On the dome is the customary band bearing the *al-asma al-husna*, or 99 Beautiful Names of God, on which rest four lotus tree-like motifs, one of which is inscribed with the *shahada*, or Profession of Faith. Behind the rear *qibla* façade of the saint's tomb is the six-domed, totally modernised mosque.

Not far from the modern ring road that encircles Gulbarga, and to the north of Gulbarga Fort, stands a *dargah* complex consisting of the Langarki, or Charitable Kitchen mosque (*c.* 1420), together with a number of tombs, a *jama'at khana* and an *idgah* platform. Unlike the other *dargahs* of Gulbarga, the Langarki complex does not seem to have been housed within a walled enclosure. Beautifully decorated with Quranic inscriptions and floral themes, the mosque here comprises a prayer hall with a transverse vault running parallel to the *qibla* wall and two projecting spaces. A square chamber on the north has a dome

Langarki mosque
interior, c. 1420

Mihrab, Langarki
mosque

supported on honeycomb-like *muqarnas* pendentives (the only such other example in Gulbarga is at the tomb of Firuz Shah). A later, long-hall addition, possibly for meditation, lies to the south. The transverse arches flanking the *mihrab* divide the vaulted ceiling of the hall into three zones, each covered with plaster ribs imitating timber architecture. The entire mosque is inscribed with the *al-Kahf* sura from the Quran. The *mihrab* of the Langarki mosque is one of the most elaborately decorated examples from the Bahmani period. It comprises three sets of receding and diminishing pointed arches. The first and second sets of arches repeat those on the other wall surfaces; the third, smaller set of arches has five lobes that frame the vault of the *mihrab*. The *mihrab's* vaulted semicircular niche, or "conch", is carried on temple-like colonnettes, behind which lies the diminutive recess, the whole composition emphasising qualities of depth and recess. On the roof above the *mihrab* projection is a small *chhatri*, which can be reached by steps located near to the square domed room on the northern side of the mosque. Adjoining this square domed room is a dilapidated building that probably once served as a pilgrims' hostel. Its central opening frames a corridor leading to the *idgah* on its southwestern side, thus visually and axially connecting the hostel and the *idgah* to the elaborate and beautifully decorated tomb on its eastern side.

Of the two mausolea in the Langarki complex, only the one with ornate façades is accessible to visitors (ask for the guardian with a key); the other is permanently closed. Marking the position of the *mihrab* on the southwestern façade of the accessible tomb is a lobed and echoing arched theme with a hanging ornament. Quranic inscriptions adorn the walls and *mihrab* inside; one band on the dome carries the *al-asma al-husna*, and four standing lotus-tree-like motifs.

EAST OF THE CITY

On the eastern fringe of Gulbarga lies the second, later royal funerary complex of the Bahmani sultans. Known as Haft Gumbad, or Seven Tombs, this complex comprises a number of mausolea perfectly aligned on either side of a short avenue that originally terminated in a lake, now mostly dried up. The mausolea are raised on low platforms and arranged in chronological sequence west-to-east, with the last tomb commemorating Firuz Shah at the eastern end.

The first funerary structure to be built here was the tomb of Alauddin Mujahid (d. 1378). This sultan was refused permission by Sheikh Junaidi to build his mausoleum next to that of his father

The Haft Gumbad, or Seven Tombs, 1378–1422 (Photo by Tony Korner)

in the earlier royal funerary compound since he seems to have
followed another spiritual advisor in the *dargah* at Khuldabad in
Maharashtra. Alauddin Mujahid's tomb adheres to the style of
earlier mausolea, with unadorned sloping walls, parapet of merlons
and flanged *guldastas*. The poorly preserved interior repeats well-
established early Bahmani models, with pointed and stilted arches,

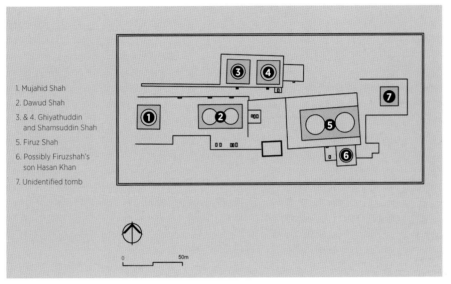

1. Mujahid Shah

2. Dawud Shah

3. & 4. Ghiyathuddin
   and Shamsuddin Shah

5. Firuz Shah

6. Possibly Firuzshah's
   son Hasan Khan

7. Unidentified tomb

Haft Gumbad plan

leaf-shaped merlons, and horseshoe-shaped arched squinches
supporting the dome, set low on the wall. The *mihrab*, set within
echoing arches, is decorated with lobed motifs; within is a conch
and roundel. There are five cenotaphs in this tomb, two constructed
of rubble stone and plastered, their bases decorated with square
panels housing geometric and floral motifs.

Alauddin Mujahid's successor, Dawud I, was murdered in
1378, on his way to Gulbarga's *Jami Masjid* (probably the Shah
Bazaar Mosque) for Friday prayers, at the instigation of Ruparwur
Agha, Alauddin Mujahid's powerful sister. Dawud I's mausoleum
introduces a Timurid architectural type, the double tomb, even
though otherwise it adheres to those of his predecessors. In the first
chamber is the burial place of the sultan; in the second chamber,
three unidentified cenotaphs. The *mihrab* is decorated in plaster,
with the word Allah, the *shahada*, and the litany of the Beautiful
Names of God.

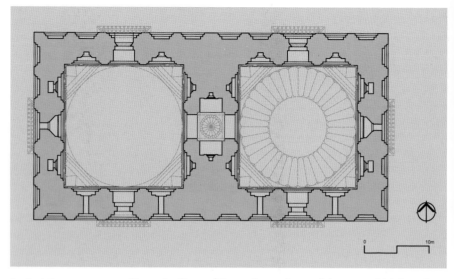

Tomb of Firuz Shah, 1422

Opposite Dawud I's tomb are those of the sons of Mahmud I, Ghiyathuddin and Shamsuddin, each of whom reigned for only a few months in 1397. In one of their tombs, the well-preserved *mihrab* continues the themes and designs noted earlier, with rosettes, lotus foliations, the *shahada*, invocations, and part of the litany of the Beautiful Names of God. Returning to the raised platform on which the Dawud I's tomb is sited, visitors will notice a number of beautifully carved dolerite gravestones in the open space connecting his tomb and that of Firuz Shah.

The tomb of Firuz Shah (d. 1422) represents the climax of the early phase of Bahmani funerary architecture. The building testifies to the ingenuity of this sultan, his varied interests and extensive knowledge. The vertical walls, which are introduced for the first time here, are divided into two tiers of recessed niches with echoing stilted arches. Their surfaces were once covered with *jalis*, as suggested by the surviving examples on the eastern façade. Above all the openings, and in front of the (recently created) *mihrab* window on the western face are basalt *chhajjas* carried on brackets, with half-pyramidal vaults. Trilobed merlons and flanged *guldastas* screen the base of the hemispherical domes. All the arched surfaces are decorated with lotus foliation, knotted patterns and inscriptions. On the southern entrance to the second chamber of the tomb is a pair of parakeets or peacocks linked by a knotted

Detail of the
southern entrance
decorated with
lotus foliations,
knotted patterns
and a parakeet,
tomb of Firuz Shah

pattern, their heads turned away towards their tails. The interior of
Firuz Shah's mausoleum is accessed via the northern entrance of its
western chamber. Here the sultan's own tomb is positioned under
a petalled dome embellished with concentric bands, two of which
carry Quranic inscriptions. The petals are decorated with hanging
ornaments, a motif that was to become popular in both Bidar and
Bijapur. The inscribed band at the base of the dome runs across
these fluted petals; on it are all of the Beautiful Names of God.
On this band sit eight "lotus-tree" motifs instead of the usual four
encountered in elite and Sufi tombs, signifying the importance of
this ruler. At the base of the dome is a *muqarnas* design. The interior
walls of the tomb chamber repeat the two-tiered arrangement of the
outer façade. On the lower register are recessed arches in multiple
receding planes, culminating in a small niche. The second arch

has five deep-plunging lobes, from which hang banana-bud motifs. On the upper register echoing arches frame *jalis* with geometric designs; the cusps of the squinches supporting the dome take the form of fluted trefoils. The five-sided *mihrab* in the western walls is inscribed with Quranic verses. Smaller niches, probably intended to store books, are inscribed with the invocation: And God is the Best Keeper and the most Merciful of Merciful.

An elaborately decorated corridor connects the western and eastern chambers of Firuz Shah's double tomb. Here, *iwan*-like areas on raised platforms have arched niches framed by ornamental bands, merlons and lotus-tree designs on their end walls. The roof of this corridor displays *muqarnas* pendentives that support an overlapping-lotus-petalled dome. The eastern chamber resembles the western chamber but is more sparsely decorated. On its walls are the same arched formations, while a lotus-tree motif has been added on the squinches. Here, too, the walls are inscribed with verses from Quranic suras, though these differ from those in the western chamber. Remains of coloured pigments can be discerned under layers of bat guano.

The palette employed by Bahmani artists can be better

View of the *dargah* of Gesu Daraz from the *dargah* of Sheikh Mujarrad

perceived in the adjacent tomb to the south, possibly that of Firuz Shah's unlucky son, Hassan Khan, who was blinded and exiled to Firuzabad by Ahmad Shah. In this tomb the same decorative themes appear as in Firuz Shah's tomb, as do a number of Quranic verses and the Beautiful Names of God. The last, unattributed mausoleum in the Haft Gumbad complex is at a lower level than the other tombs, being situated close to the original lake shore. It is decorated with foliate motifs, the word Allah, Quranic inscriptions, and the *shahada*.

On leaving the Haft Gumbad, visitors should take the road running around the north side of the lake to reach the *dargah* of Gesu Daraz, signposted as the KBN *Dargah*. This road is built on a barrage that originally separated two interconnected lakes: one at the end of the Haft Gumbad complex just described; and another lake where are located the three monumental Noor Bagh tombs sharing a single platform. These unattributed mausolea are associated with an ornamental step-well that can be seen just below one of the tombs.

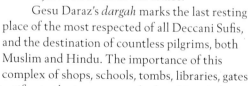

Gesu Daraz's *dargah* marks the last resting place of the most respected of all Deccani Sufis, and the destination of countless pilgrims, both Muslim and Hindu. The importance of this complex of shops, schools, tombs, libraries, gates

Tomb of Gesu Daraz, one of the most respected Deccani Sufis, 15th century and later

and prayer halls, testifies to the important role that this saintly figure played in establishing Islam in the region and to his enduring popularity. Gesu Daraz was invited to settle in Gulbarga by Firuz Shah. Relations between Sufi and sultan were initially amicable, but their opposing religious, political and social views led to an estrangement, and Gesu Daraz was "banished" from the city by being granted the land where his *dargah* is presently located. It was here that Ahmad Shah became his *murid*. After the saint's death

in 1423 the sultan erected an impressive mausoleum for his spiritual advisor.

The *dargah* compound is accessed by modern concrete steps leading to a visitors' entrance near a recently built mosque. Gesu Daraz's tomb is a monumental structure that shares a number of features with that of Firuz Shah, some 500 metres away. The power of this shrine continued during the successor dynasties, in particular under the Adil Shahis. The interior was subjected to insensitive renovation in the 1950s with mirror work that

Tombs in the *dargah* of Gesu Daraz

recalls Rajasthani palace decoration rather than traditional Deccani motifs. Certain details follow the same configuration as those of Firuz Shah's mausoleum, notably the five-faceted *mihrab*, the fluted trefoil squinches, the dome designs and the Quranic inscriptions and litany of holy names.

Immediately opposite Gesu Daraz's tomb is the equally impressive, monumental mausoleum of the saint's beloved son Sayyid Akbar Hussaini (d. 1409). Surrounding the gate of this tomb is a Quranic inscription and Shi'i texts probably belonging to the Adil Shahi period. Dating from more recent times are the paintings that decorate the wall of the interior and recall those in the tomb of Ahmad Shah at Ashtur. On the southwestern side of Gesu Daraz's mausoleum is another tomb belonging to one of his sons; beyond it stand lesser tombs dating from the 16th and 17th centuries.

The funerary edifices just described are aligned along a path in a manner resembling that at the Haft Gumbad. To the northeast of Sayyid Akbar Hussaini's tomb is a domed passage leading to a lower-level courtyard, around which are disposed some of the most interesting buildings in the *dargah*. Facing the domed gateway is a ceremonial arch framed by two square towers with openings on four levels and overhanging *chhajjas*. A gallery over this arch is decorated with leaf-shaped merlons; below these is a

Ceremonial arch to the water reservoir from the *dargah* of Gesu Daraz, 17th and 18th centuries

line of openings for pigeons. On the spandrels are brackets with roundels depicting elephants carrying lions. This ceremonial arch, which once framed the lake beyond, probably dates from the 17th century, as do the other buildings around the courtyard, which include rooms for pilgrims, a library and a small mosque. Below the arch, the small chamber with a curved vaulted roof recalls Mughal architecture, as do the designs of fruits on platters that adorn its façade. The library and mosque, with its overhanging *chhajjas* on brackets, chain ornaments and domed *guldastas*, are assigned to the Adil Shahi period.

To reach the *dargah* of Sheikh Mujarrad, another Sufi patronised by Firuz Shah, visitors should return to the Haft Gumbad (described above) and drive around the lake to a hill on its eastern side. The *dargah* here includes a number of *baolis*, one located below the *qibla* wall of the mosque. These features indicate that the complex was once surrounded by gardens and arable lands, probably gifted to the saint by Firuz Shah. The buildings associated with the tomb of this figure, whose death date is unknown, include a mosque, an elegant structure with an awning on stone columns, possibly for the saint's followers, and, immediately to the east, a long multi-domed structure with small rooms to accommodate pilgrims and *murids*. As Sheikh Mujarrad was one of Firuz Shah's spiritual advisors, it is probable that this sultan also patronised the construction of the *dargah*. This is suggested by the elaborate ornamentation found in its mosque, which is the best-preserved building in the complex. The five arched façade of the fifteen-bay mosque, with a *chhajja* (now vanished) supported on carved stone brackets, was once distinguished by inscribed lobed arches that no longer survive. The central *mihrab* is decorated with a heart-shaped tree motif, on both sides of which are two roundels containing the word Allah and lines from Quranic verse 61.

SOUTH OF THE FORT

Along the main road connecting KBN *Dargah* to Gulbarga city are two imposing tombs built next to each other on the same platform, with a nearby well. Each tomb is entered from the south; the other entrances are now blocked up. Their interiors are decorated with customary vegetal and winged motifs on the apex of arches bearing the word Allah. On the roundels of the northern openings, visitors

External view of *qibla* wall of the mosque in the *dargah* of Sheikh Mujarrad, c. 1410

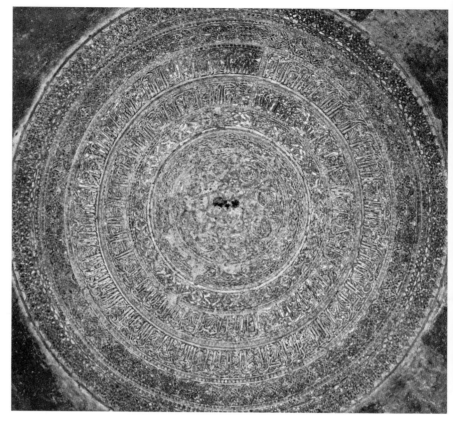

Carved stucco design on the inside of the dome of the Gubbi colony tomb, *c.* 1410

will see the invocation *Ya Allah*. The *mihrab* arches have been covered by layers of plaster, and the reading of their designs and inscriptions is now difficult.

Continuing through the southern section of the city, visitors will reach the tombs in the colonies of Santraswadi and Gubbi located southeast of Gulbarga Fort. The three mausolea in Santraswadi, one unfinished, date from the late-14th century. Within the conch of the *mihrab* in each tomb is a roundel with a cross-shaped pattern, the arms of which are inscribed with the *kalima*, or Confession of Faith. Also associated with these tombs is a *baoli*. Its stone pulleys are still visible, as are the remains of stone conduits to distribute the water around the gardens that once surrounded the tombs. These probably formed part of an asymmetrical landscape with groves of mangoes, tamarinds and

Lotus-tree motif in one of the squinches of the Gubbi colony tomb

coconut trees. The Gubbi Colony tomb, dating from the early-15th century, is lavishly decorated. It stands on a wide platform that was once surrounded by gardens, as implied by the nearby *baoli*. Foliate designs embellish the southern door and southeast squinch; the other squinches and the *mihrab* are inscribed with the *kalima*, the Beautiful Names of God and Quranic verses. On the band at the base of the dome are four lotus-tree motifs; the dome's apex displays concentric bands of inscriptions and lotus scrolls on which the remains of red, blue, grey-black and aquamarine pigments can be seen. The impressive *baoli*, which is still in use, is rectangular in layout, with a flight of steps descending down to a walkway that runs around the well. On its western side is an original pointed arch (the two other openings are recent). The platform on its southern edge widens to accommodate temple-like columns for the pulley.

View of the royal
villa at Sultanpur,
c. 1410

SULTANPUR

About 5 kilometres northwest of Gulbarga Fort is Sultanpur, the King's Village. This locality is mentioned in historical sources as the place where the sultan would alight on his way to the western provinces of the Bahmani kingdom. The royal villa at Sultanpur occupies an area where the sultan's agricultural lands were probably situated. This is suggested by the surrounding hydraulic works, including an ornamental step-well on its northwestern side. Other wells, canals and bridges testify to a sophisticated irrigation system that once serviced the surrounding farmlands.

Design with birds
on the apex of an
arch in the royal
villa

The Sultanpur villa comprises two wings framing a central space defined by a pattern of 3 by 3 bays. The projecting wings are

smaller and comprise 3 by 2 bays. On the southern side of the central space of the villa is an opening to accommodate a timber balcony (now vanished); a similar arrangement was at its western end, indicating both north-south and east-west alignments for the building. A flight of stairs climbing to the roof, covered by a stepped vault set within the northwestern wall, divides the central room from the western room. Pairs of birds, their heads turned towards their tails, adorn the apex of an arch.

The remains of a congregational mosque are seen a short distance along the main road, east of the villa. These comprise a domed, square gateway and wall segments of a prayer hall.

FIRUZABAD

The ruins of the royal city of Firuzabad lie 30 kilometres from Gulbarga beside the highway running south from the city, just before the road bridge across the Bhima river. Before diverting to modern-day Firuzabad village, next to which are the ruins of this ancient metropolis, visitors are urged to stop at the *dargah* of Khalifat al-Rahman, an enigmatic saint about whom nothing is known, situated next to the main road about 2 kilometres from the ruins.

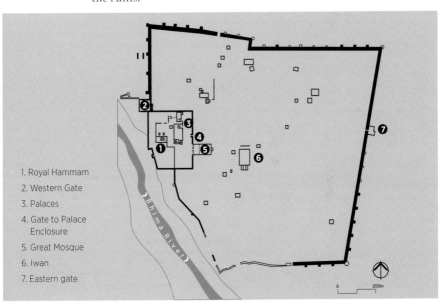

1. Royal Hammam
2. Western Gate
3. Palaces
4. Gate to Palace
   Enclosure
5. Great Mosque
6. Iwan
7. Eastern gate

Firuzabad

Khalifat al-Rahman's *dargah* was built by Firuz Shah Bahmani, probably *c.* 1410. The complex consists of an elegant, cross-in-square tomb and a mosque, between which is a deep, square well carved out of the rock. The *dargah* exhibits several unique features. Deccani Islamic burials are usually located under a dome, but this edifice contains two burials: one in the eastern *iwan* and the other in the southeast corner of the central domed space. These unique locations and the cross-in-square layout suggest that the burials may be later insertions and that the building is best understood as a royal audience hall rather than a tomb. The adjacent mosque accords to the well-known congregational type, with a domed gate opening into a courtyard with a prayer hall at its southwestern end. Attached to the northwest side of this mosque is a funerary chamber with its own entrance, possibly for the grave of Abdul Rahman; if so, this would be the only Bahmani funerary mosque. In recent years, the mosque has been rebuilt in concrete and the burial chamber obliterated. Two stone

Western gate, Firuzabad, c. 1400

inscriptions are seen in front of the mosque's gateway. One states that the supervisor for the construction of the *Jami Masjid* in nearby Firuzabad, completed in 1406, was Ahmad son of Husain al-Hisn Kaifi (a city close to Diyarbakir in modern-day Turkey); the other is an epitaph of Khwaja Shamsuddin al-Rumi, a resident of Bursa (also in Turkey), who died here in 1421.

The royal city of Firuzabad is located on the left bank of the Bhima river, beside a small village, reached by a side road that leads off the highway running beside the *dargah* just described. Firuz Shah started building Firuzabad in 1399, one year after his enthronement. The tour of Firuzabad will take several hours and requires good walking shoes and long trousers, as the terrain is rough and the vegetation prickly. This city is quadrangular in layout, being defined by defensive stone walls with gates located at the four cardinal points. The eastern and western gates are the more

Remains of a *hammam* in the city, c. 1400

sophisticated entryways. The eastern walls have special openings framing the gate, implying the use of firearms. Additional walls enclose a rectangle with rooms and a protected curved entrance path (currently with a fallen arch), suggesting that this was a secure area for overnight visitors or merchants. Along the stone path to the eastern gateway are collapsed walls, domes and temple-like columns, as well as small square structures with pyramidal vaults, denoting the former existence of numerous buildings. Where this path bends, visitors will encounter the remains of a *hammam*.

Lions/tigers in plaster relief on the gate leading to the royal enclosure, c. 1400

This comprised two adjoining domed square chambers, the first framed by lesser chambers with pyramidal vaults. Trilobed arched designs, *muqarnas*-type pendentives, the remains of fluted domes, plaster-lined flues set into the walls, and holes to admit light in the partly-brick-built domes are all features that testify to the ingenuity of the builders who introduced this new building type and constructional technique into the Deccan. Northeast of this *hammam* are two *baolis*, and beyond them several structures with ribbed vaults of uncertain purpose.

Turning south, visitors may now follow another path which is bordered by fields. Along it stands an impressive gateway, which once gave access to the palace enclosure. Here it was no longer bastions and guards that protected the palace quarter, but depictions of walking lions or tigers in plaster relief. Instead of passing into the royal enclosure, however, visitors should continue towards a two-storeyed structure with a double-height chamber and four transverse arches, probably for a timber roof that has now disappeared. One of the most conspicuous ceremonial halls in Firuzabad, the structure faces north towards an area that unfolds in front of the *Jami Masjid*; to the south, it opens onto a rectangular

space that could have accommodated a tent, thus further enlarging the building's original floor plan.

Visitors should now enter the *Jami Masjid*, possibly one of the largest examples of a congregational mosque in the Deccan. Following well established Bahmani traditions, the mosque has a domed gateway, its walls faced with finely carved basalt. The large rectangular courtyard within is framed on the north and west by walls with tall arched openings. Little remains of the prayer hall, however. Only the peripheral walls and a few corner domes remain of its 13 by 5 bays; debris from fallen construction conceals much of the interior. The *mihrabs* along the *qibla* wall, embellished with foliate motifs, mark the ends of the perpendicular aisles. A stepped, stone *minbar* adjoins the central main *mihrab*, beside which is a

Dome, with *muqarnas* pendentives in the *hammam* of the royal enclosure

doorway leading directly to the palace area to the rear. On the northern side of the prayer hall, two doorways at different levels are connected to a staircase and an intermediate level where the *muluk khana* was located.

Visitors can reach the palace area by scrambling through the small opening beside the *minbar* (if it is not filled with stones); otherwise, they should return to the monumental arched gateway with the walking animal motifs. The palace area is framed on three sides by the city of Firuzabad itself, its southwestern side abutting the sands of the Bhima river's bank. Here visitors will encounter a number of fallen buildings, some of them double-storeyed with broad transverse arches. The best preserved structure here is a *hammam*, which displays a cluster of differently-sized domes and pyramidal vaults. Unlike the example already described, this bath is entered via a small doorway on its southeastern corner, which leads to a line of three domed chambers. The central chamber opens into a large square-domed space, from which visitors may access square side chambers roofed with pyramidal vaults, and a rectangular pool to the west. Geometric and foliate plaster motifs and fluted domes on *muqarnas* pendentives are among the many well preserved designs to be seen here.

Returning to the village of Firuzabad, visitors may admire the west gateway of the city, with its walls defining a square enclosure. These gateways were checkpoints, controlling the flow of visitors and goods. The square rooms found here probably accommodated the guards and clerks that resided here.

HOLKONDA

The small settlement of Holkonda, some 20 kilometres northeast of Gulbarga on the road to Bidar (look out for the sign beside the road), is worth visiting for its unusual group of tombs dating from the Bahmani period. In the village there is a gate that resembles those of Firuzabad, but the site's most important feature is an

Tombs on the hilltop of Holkonda, 14th and 15th centuries

View of the funerary platform that adjoins the water reservoir at Holkonda

impressive funerary compound on a hill, which is entered through its own monumental gate. Its arched recessed façade and ribs decorating its interior vault recall similar features at Firuzabad. On both sides of the entrance are small kiosks covered by lotus-shaped domes sheltering deeply carved stone water containers for pilgrims.

Different types of tombs found at Holkonda suggest that the funerary complex here was built over a period of some 80-100 years. The mausoleum on the southern platform and the whitewashed mausoleum of Sheikh Masha'ikh are the two earliest edifices, probably dating from the late-14th century. (Masha'ikh is a generic term for saint, and is also given to anonymous buried figures after they have attained saintly status.) Of the other tombs, one is octagonal, and resembles mid-15th-century examples; the remaining tombs have their surfaces decorated with two tiers of arched niches, thus resembling those at Ashtur. Two additional, brick built tombs stand outside the walled enclosure, behind the *qibla* wall of a mosque. The five tombs inside the compound as well as these two examples are aligned on axis with the mosque's main *mihrab*. This is the only Deccani mosque to be divided into three units by arches carried on timber columns.

Outside the northwestern corner of the funerary compound is the finest *baoli* from the early Bahmani period. Its trilobed squinches indicate a date in the early-15th century. Openings in the compound's southern wall suggest that the hilltop compound and platform below were linked in some way. This stone platform was located within a reservoir and surrounded by a semicircular

Baoli from the
early Bahmani
period, Holkonda,
c. 1400

earthen dam that began northwest of the platform, and continued
along its southeastern side. On the platform is a domed pavilion
carried on reused temple columns, an *idgah* and an open-air burial
framed by a *jali* fence.

BIDAR

PRECEDING PAGES:
Bidar Fort, Tarkash Mahal, c. 1480

Ahmad Shah, brother and successor of Firuz Shah, moved the capital of the Bahmani kingdom from Gulbarga to Bidar in 1432. This relocation achieved a number of economic and political goals. Bidar borders an area rich in agricultural and mineral resources and strategically positioned on the trans-peninsular commercial corridor linking the eastern and western seaboards. With this move, Ahmad Shah also distanced himself from the courtly intrigues of Gulbarga and the partisan role played by the *dargah* belonging to Gesu Daraz, his *pir*, or spiritual adviser, who died in 1423. To emphasise this break with the past and his independence from Sufi sects, with their well-established local power structures, Ahmad Shah invited Shah Nimatullah to come from Iran to become his spiritual preceptor in Bidar. Shah Nimatullah himself was unable to accept this generous invitation, owing to his advanced years, but his family did. The Nimatullahis integrated into the royal family through repeated marriages with Bahmani princesses, while the generosity of Ahmad Shah and his successors provided them with substantial landholdings in Nimatabad near Bidar, and Beer further north.

Plan of Bidar city and Fort

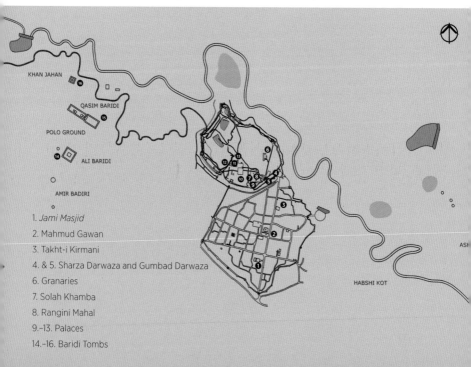

KHAN JAHAN

QASIM BARIDI

POLO GROUND

ALI BARIDI

AMIR BADIRI

1. *Jami Masjid*
2. Mahmud Gawan
3. Takht-i Kirmani
4. & 5. Sharza Darwaza and Gumbad Darwaza
6. Granaries
7. Solah Khamba
8. Rangini Mahal
9.–13. Palaces
14.–16. Baridi Tombs

HABSHI KOT

ASH

Bidar was a planned city combining the quadrangular plan of Firuzabad, the royal foundation near Gulbarga, with the circular layout of Warangal and Devagiri-Daulatabad. This quadrangular part of Bidar accommodated the administrative and religious buildings of the city as well as the dwellings of its inhabitants, while

the fort to which it was attached served as the headquarters, with a royal enclosure and a number of auxiliary service buildings such as granaries. City and fort were linked by the Sharza Darwaza. East of the fort lay Habshi Kot or Habshi quarter, while to the northeast was the necropolis of Ashtur, where the Bahmani sultans and the Nimatullahis are buried. The Bahmanis' royal camp lay to the west of the fort, while further westwards were the tombs of the Baridi sultans and their polo ground. The Baridis inherited Bidar and its surroundings on the dissolution of the Bahmani kingdom at the turn of the 16th century. Two royal suburbs are associated with Bidar: Nimatabad and Kamthana. Nimatabad, built on the bank of the Manjuri river, was evidently of some importance judging from the heaps of rubble and ruined walls with embedded pink-granite columns that may still be seen. A reservoir, a barrage and the remains of a gate testify to the status of Kamthana as an important suburb southwest of Bidar.

View of the walled fort with moat, Bidar, c. 1430

The tour of Bidar starts within the city and proceeds to the fort where the royal enclosure is located. It then leaves the city to visit the necropolis of Ashtur, approximately 6 kilometres east of the fort, and the shrine of Fakhr al-Mulk in Fathpur, on the way to Nimatabad, 7 kilometres northeast of the fort. West of Bidar city stand the tombs of the Baridi sultans, and on the way to Hyderabad is the famous Chishti *Dargah* of Abu'l Faid, the final stop on the tour.

THE WALLED CITY

The city of Bidar is protected by a glacis, or artificial slope, to keep assailants under fire, as well as a moat and impressive stone fortifications with merlons reinforced with circular and pentagonal bastions. The loopholed battlements of the ramparts testify to the use of muskets and other firearms, while on the bastions cannons can still be seen. Visitors can follow the passage behind the battlements to further explore the impressive defences and artillery installed by successive rulers who made Bidar their headquarters.

Bidar's fortifications mostly date from the second half of the 15th century, when Mahmud Gawan ordered an overhaul of the city walls so as to deal with the newly introduced gunpowder and cannon. These improvements were probably undertaken during the

The mid-15th-century *Jami Masjid, c.* 1480

prosperous reign of Muhammad Shah (r. 1463–82). Further upgrading of the city defences were initiated after the battle of Talikota (1565), during the reign of Ali Shah Baridi (r. 1543–80) who participated in the downfall of the Vijayanagara kingdom. Under the Adil Shahis in the 17th century, Bidar's city walls were repaired by the residing representative of the Bijapuri rulers. The Mughals further strengthened the urban defences after they captured Bidar in 1656, and the Asaf Jahis continued this tradition.

Mihrab in *Jami Masjid*

The city tour will begin at the Nauras, or Fath Darwaza, on the southern walls, where the Hyderabad road ends. Visitors can follow the north-south road that runs through the city to the mid-15th-century *Chaubara* (four-fold house), a tower-like structure, with a staircase leading to the top. This stands at the crossroads of Bidar's two principal thoroughfares, indicating that the city originally followed a grid plan. The commanding views of Bidar and its surrounding area from the top of *Chaubara* suggest that it served as an observation point. From here it would have been possible to monitor hostile activities outside the walls, as well as within the walls between the Afaqis and Dakhinis. From the *Chaubara* visitors can return towards the Fath Darwaza and take a small lane running west of the main north-south road in order to reach the city's mid-15th-century *Jami Masjid*. This partly adheres to the layout of a typical Bahmani congregational mosque, though the square gate pavilion to the courtyard is missing. Southwest of this courtyard is the prayer hall with its imposing seven-arched façade. Its central, largest arch opens onto the aisle ending in front of the main seven-sided *mihrab*, now painted in the most abject colours. The surfaces of the arched façade display plaster designs of vases and oval medallions filled with dense scrolls, recalling patterns found on late Bahmani and Baridi monuments in the royal enclosure.

Returning to *Chaubara*, visitors should continue along the north-south road until they arrive at what is perhaps the most important and unusual building of Bidar, the monumental *madrasa*

The monumental madrasa of Mahmud Gawan, built in 1472

of Mahmud Gawan, built in 1472. This figure travelled from Iran to Bidar during the reign of Allauddin Shah (r. 1436–58), to sit at the feet of one of the descendants of Shah Nimatullah. He arrived bearing important gifts and also horses for sale, the most desirable commodity in the Deccan during the entire sultanate period. Mahmud Gawan's intelligence and political acumen contributed to his meteoric rise at the Bahmani court; according to Humayun Shah Bahmani (r. 1458–61), "he was well known the world over, and excelled in wisdom among the Arabs as well as the Persians". Belonging to Bidar's Afaqi community, Mahmud Gawan attempted to resolve the constant strife with the Dakhinis. During his long viziership (1461–82), he tried to balance both communities politically by placing their representatives as governors of the same districts and as commanders of military expeditions.

Mahmud Gawan's *madrasa* is deeply indebted to the Timurid architectural traditions of Central Asia and is unique in India. Part of its southern façade was destroyed in 1696, either by lightning or by gunpowder that was stored in its premises during the Mughal occupation. Of its imposing eastern façade, only the northern corner survives, with its arcaded openings and corner, cylindrical minarets cloaked in brilliantly coloured tile mosaics. This decoration was most likely executed by immigrant craftsmen from Uzbekistan or Iran. Steps on the east lead to the central square courtyard, where three out of four *iwans* topped by domes on high drums survive. The lofty portals are framed by three tiers of arches that lead to apartments for students and their teachers. Some of the apartments have a raised passage with a small vaulted area, which is just large enough to permit someone to sit in and was probably used for meditation.

On leaving the *madrasa*, visitors should turn north and continue along the road towards the fort. Soon they will see the west-facing façade of the Takht-i Kirmani (c.1500). This impressive gateway has a recessed double-arched entrance framed by two tiers of arched windows and with leaf-merlon finials. The façade is beautifully decorated in stucco with flowering vases, roundels with radiating mirror calligraphy, and other vegetal themes. Within the inner, recessed arched entrance, where niches define the surface of the wall, a plaster depiction of a lion figure with a raised paw can be made out. The gateway was probably the entrance to a quarter occupied by immigrants from Kirman, the Iranian birthplace of Shah Nimatullah; hence its name. From here visitors should now continue to the Sharza Darwaza and the entrance to Bidar Fort.

The arched entrance of the Takht-i Kirmani depicting a lion figure with a raised paw, c. 1480

BIDAR FORT

The first gate encountered when arriving from the city is the Sharza Darwaza, which is an amalgamation of different gateways. Its arched entrance with two small turrets dates from the Mughal period (late-17th century), and originally had a drawbridge, since replaced by a road. A courtyard connects this gateway to another court and to the Sharza Darwaza, with its polygonal towers with balconies and sculpted lion figures in high relief, after which the gate takes its name.

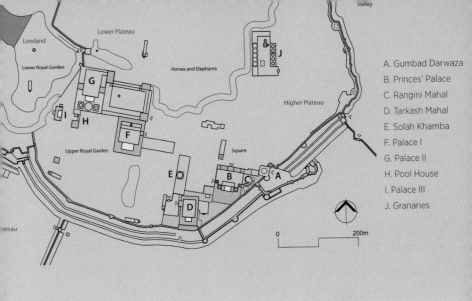

Lower Plateau

Lowland

Lower Royal Garden

G

Horses and Elephants

J

Higher Plateau

H

F

Upper Royal Garden

Square

E

B **C** **A**

D

ateau

A. Gumbad Darwaza
B. Princes' Palace
C. Rangini Mahal
D. Tarkash Mahal
E. Solah Khamba
F. Palace I
G. Palace II
H. Pool House
I. Palace III
J. Granaries

0   200m

Plan of Bidar Fort
A beautiful inscription engraved on grey basalt mentions its date of construction as 1503, during Mahmud Shah's reign (r. 1482–1518). Further embellishments in polychrome tilework can be seen above this inscription.

Passing through the Sharza Darwaza, visitors will cross the wide road running over the moat to reach the Gumbad Darwaza; on the way they may admire the magnificent prospect of fortification walls, bastions and rock-cut moats. The moat to the left of this road becomes a triple ditch. Above rise the beautifully built ramparts that shield the palaces in the fort's southwestern segment. From the windows set into the palaces walls, the inhabitants could admire the gardens that once existed in certain areas of the moat. These magnificent ramparts date from Ahmad Shah's reign (c. 1430) and employ reused temple columns of pink granite, as well as funerary Muslim inscriptions and basalt stonework.

Beneath the soaring dome of the square Gumbad Darwaza, an octagonal space opens onto a large courtyard that leads to the royal enclosure of the fort. Doors protected the frontal (eastern) entrance, which is framed by monumental circular bastions, later additions, suggesting that originally this was a free-standing pavilion used for royal ceremonies. Under the apex of the lofty pointed arch on its frontal façade is an arched window that once overlooked the esplanade, now occupied by the approach road from the Sharza Darwaza. The octagonal chamber inside the Gumbad

Bidar fort. View
of the Gumbad
Darwaza, entrance
to the royal
enclosure, *c.* 1430

Arched niches on
the interior of the
Gumbad Darwaza,
c. 1430

Darwaza has eight tall arched niches and two windows on the south and north. These windows illuminate small square rooms with pyramidal vaults. Remains of painted decoration on the dome indicate that the same painters may have worked in this building as in Ahmad Shah's tomb at Ashtur.

Steps immediately to the west of the Gumbad Darwaza lead to a door that opens into a courtyard with the remains of a Mughal-type landscaped garden (ask the guardian for the key). This gives direct access to the Rangini Mahal, the best-preserved palace in Bidar, of particular interest for its partly wooden construction and sumptuous decoration. The palace has a north-facing tripartite façade, the central part of which comprises a *mandapa*, or columned hall. The square timber columns of this hall support a beautifully carved wooden ceiling carried on wooden brackets with pendant banana-bud motifs derived from local Hindu architecture. The rear walls of the hall are decorated with 16th-17th century underglaze-painted tiles depicting foliate designs and flowering vases. The panels are framed by basalt colonnettes inlaid with mother-of-pearl. The doorway in the middle of the rear wall leads to a room that overlooks the moat. Its doorway is adorned with exquisite spiralling scrolls of mother of pearl inlaid into basalt as well as amorous and spiritual verses. It may have served for Ali Baridi's recreational activities. Unique to Bidar, this inlay work may be considered amongst the finest of all Deccani decorative arts. The arched space on the northern side of the Rangini Mahal's courtyard is decorated with vegetal and bird designs in plaster relief, in which small pieces of turquoise tiles were inlaid to highlight the effect of the design. One of the domed chambers adjoining this area is painted with radiating motifs that recall the themes of Persian carpets. These chambers may date from the reign of Mahmud Shah Bahmani.

One can now return to the plaza with the banyan tree. Further on from the steps leading to the Rangini Mahal is a line of arches belonging to domed spaces, now practically inaccessible. Just before

Rangini Mahal,
the best-preserved
palace in Bidar,
c. 1500 and later

The carved wooden ceiling in the *mandapa* of the Rangini Mahal

visitors reach a tall enclosure wall topped by merlons in the form of cut-out intersecting arches, they will see the 15th-century imposing façade of the Prince's Palace, intended as the residence for the heir to the Bahmani throne. This façade comprises a large arch framed by two arched niches with embedded 17th-century Adil Shahi inscriptions. The Prince's Palace has undergone various alterations, and served both as a prison and a kitchen during the Asaf Jahi period. The ceremonial section of the palace, with its tripartite façade, to the south of the courtyard is presently obscured by later constructions. Doors once protected the seven-sided apsidal hall within, which was decorated with intersecting arched motifs and chain ornaments, all in plaster. On both sides of this hall are cross-in-square-plan rooms with tall domes. Framing this ceremonial section are two projecting towers. The rectangular tower on the east and square tower on the west are aligned with the central domed space of the Solah Khamba, the large columned hall facing onto the Mughal garden known as the Lal Bagh, west of the Prince's Palace.

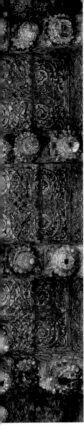

Visitors should now return to the large plaza with a spreading banyan tree to the west of the Gumbad Darwaza, and from there pass through the iron gates to enter the walled enclosure with the remains of the Mughal garden in the Lal Bagh. On the northern side of this enclosure was the Archaeological Museum that was relocated opposite the steps of the Rangini Mahal. It occupied a so-called 'hammam' even though the features of a bath are not apparent. Chalukya statuary from the 11th-12th centuries is displayed here, as well as finds from the excavations in Bidar Fort undertaken in the early-20th century.

The Lal Bagh, which unfolds in front of the Solah Khamba, was probably originally unenclosed. During the late-15th century, at the height of Bahmani supremacy, the different areas of the fort, stretching from the Gumbad Darwaza to the northwest promontory, as well as the verdant valley below the ramparts, were probably connected, permitting displays of pomp and processions worthy of the dynasty's power.

The canal that runs from the Tarkash Mahal, on the southern side of the Lal Bagh, to the almond-shaped lotus pool in the middle of the garden dates from the Mughal occupation. It was probably at this time that the basalt lobed revetment of the pool was removed from its original position in the western courtyard of the Takht Mahal (Palace II). The relocation of this revetment suggests that by the 17th century ceremonial activities within the fort were focused on the Solah Khamba and adjoining palaces.

Dome with radiating motifs in the Rangini Mahal

The identification of the Solah Khamba as a mosque dating from either 1324 or 1424 relies on an inscription found in nearby debris. Recently re-interpreted as a ceremonial audience hall, this hall originally comprised a square domed pavilion with steps up to small arched openings raised approximately 1.5 metres above the present floor level (not original). These openings were located in the walls of the pavilion's three large arches and were connected with balconies, possibly with timber *jalis*, that concealed the identity of those seated behind. Under the domed space and on the western wall of this pavilion are three arched niches aligned with the two towers of the Prince's Palace, already noticed. During the late-15th century columned halls were added, thereby converting the audience chamber into a prayer hall that could function as a mosque. This alteration is betrayed by the column in front of the eastern arch of the original pavilion, which interrupts the view from the domed space to the towers.

The next building in this part of the Bidar Fort to be described is the Tarkash Mahal. This dates from the end of the Bahmani period and that of Baridi rule. To enter, visitors must follow the exterior western wall of the Solah Khamba and enter a

The Solah Khamba facing onto the Mughal garden of Lal Bagh, c. 1460 and later

Interior of the
Solah Khamba,
with its imposing
columned halls,
c. 1460 and later

courtyard through the iron doors that are located to the southwest.
Recent restoration here has contributed to cleaner spaces, but in
the process has obliterated architectural evidence that would have
permitted a better understanding of this fascinating complex,
dating from the time of Ahmad Shah, which sits astride the
ramparts of the fort.

Recent excavations have revealed that the Tarkash Mahal and
Prince's Palace were once connected via a number of courtyards.
Mounds of fallen masonry indicate that this area was once densely
built up around a series of courtyards disposed at different levels.
The large hall on the upper storey, embellished with arched niches
and magnificent plaster designs, overlooks the esplanade of the
Solah Khamba.

The open area between the southwestern group of palaces
just described and the complex of palaces on the northwestern
promontory of Bidar Fort probably accommodated gardens, and
possibly even a tented camp, and could have functioned as an
extension of the actual palace structures. Water was provided
by the various wells that can still be seen in this upper garden
section of the fort; irrigation was further supported by the elaborate
qanat system.

Tarkash Mahal, c. 1500

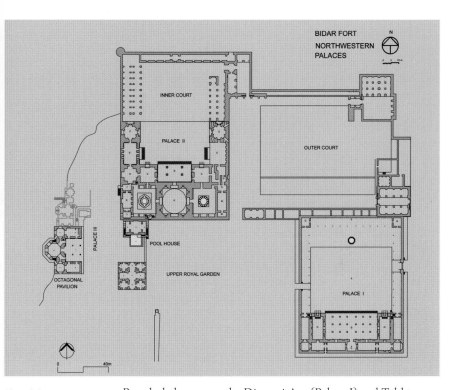

Plan of the northwestern palaces of Bidar Fort

Popularly known as the Diwan-i-Am (Palace I) and Takht Mahal (Palace II), these two complexes, located on the promontory overlooking the verdant valley below, probably fulfilled the administrative, ceremonial and residential functions of the 15th-century Bahmani court. Each complex comprises a rectangular walled courtyard, the southern side of which accommodates a north-facing palace with a tripartite façade. The two palaces shared the same decorative techniques in carved basalt and timber, polychrome underglaze tiles, and tile-mosaic ornamentation. The southern section of the Diwan-i-Am had three storeys, the uppermost one with timber balconies and views over the southwestern gardens of the fort, and temporary structures that probably once lay between it and the ramparts. Its western and eastern wings were two-storeyed, the upper level containing an open-air verandah with *jali* windows, from which the royal ladies could observe the ceremonies taking place in the surrounding areas.

Exterior of Palace I, popularly known as Diwan-i-Am, *c.* 1440

Southern columned hall of Palace I (Diwan-i-Am), *c.* 1440

Chamber behind the southern columned hall, *c.* 1440

The internal courtyard of the Diwan-i-Am is surrounded on three sides by raised platforms, with square rooms roofed with corner pyramidal vaults. The midpoint of the courtyard's northern wall was occupied by a cascading fountain. This was connected through underground channels to an octagonal pool with holes for water jets set into its dolerite revetments. Below this platform lay a sunken garden area, probably planted with fruit trees; the remaining surface of the courtyard was paved with stones. These features lie on axis with the central aisle of the columned hall to the south of the courtyard. This hall is raised on a platform reached by steps fashioned from finely finished, green basalt blocks. Large, tall timber columns, probably originally covered in gold plate, supported a timber ceiling, now altogether vanished. These, together with the polychrome underglaze tiling on the walls, must have contributed to a luxurious environment. The columned hall is connected to side rooms with overhanging timber balconies, while its central aisle opened onto a small rear chamber. This chamber must have been similarly decorated, but also had the added luxury of a geometric patterned pavement created from inlaid black-and-white marble pieces. In the centre of this floor is an octagonal recess, possibly for a portable emblem of power, such as a royal standard. The absence of a dome suggests that this palace was not a royal

ceremonial structure but rather an important administrative centre.

Several metres northwest of the Diwan-i-Am stands the Takht Mahal (or Palace II).

Palace II (Takht Mahal) northwestern tower, *c.* 1440

This complex is built up to the northwestern periphery of Bidar Fort, overlooking the gardens on the plateau below. The Takht Mahal has an inner and an outer courtyard. To reach the inner court, visitors had to pass through two gated areas. (Since these gates are now locked, visitors must enter the Takht Mahal from a small doorway on the southern side of the palace; ask the guard for the key.) On entering the Takht Mahal visitors were greeted by a blind arched façade that opens into a corridor with a raised

platform, possibly to help the descent from horseback. From there, they pass along a domed passage that opens into the inner courtyard of the complex. The rooms at the northwestern and northeastern corners of the palace originally projected forwards as two *pishtaq* towers, outwardly identical but differing internally. The northwestern tower, the only one to partly survive, contained an octagonal chamber probably with an octagonal pyramidal roof, with walls decorated with

Lion with sunburst in northwestern tower, *c.* 1440

polychrome mosaic tiles framed by basalt rods. The spandrels of the lofty pointed arches of the tower's external façade depict tigers with sunbursts.

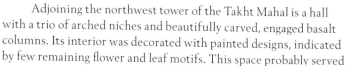

Palace II throne
room, framed
by open-air
courtyards, c. 1440

Adjoining the northwest tower of the Takht Mahal is a hall with a trio of arched niches and beautifully carved, engaged basalt columns. Its interior was decorated with painted designs, indicated by few remaining flower and leaf motifs. This space probably served

as the entrance to the western and best-preserved section of the palace. This contained a room with a mandala-like plan that probably functioned as a "distribution centre" for pedestrian movement through the western part of the palace, from where the private rooms of the sultan could be accessed. From one of these rooms, it was possible to descend to the gardens on the northwestern side of the palace and that connected Palace II with III, or Ladies Palace. The central room of the sultan's quarters in Palace II preserves traces of a fascinating cooling system, with ducts feeding out to an open-air terrace above. Adjoining these royal quarters was a courtyard with an almond-shaped lotus pool. (Its original dolerite revetment can now be seen in the similarly shaped pool in the Lal Bagh.) This courtyard is framed by tall arched niches, once adorned with polychrome tile mosaics. From here steps led to a pool house abutting the southwest corner of the complex.

Pool house on the
southwest corner
of the complex,
c. 1500

Remains of walls suggest that the eastern section of the Takht Mahal (Palace II) followed a different internal layout, even though its exterior repeated that of the western side. In the eastern section, there is another courtyard with a square pool that included a 14-petalled lotus basin. The space between these two courtyards, each housing a differently shaped water body, was the most important in all of Bidar Fort for here was located the sultan's

Octagonal pool in pool house

throne room, the dome of which could be seen from the plains of the Manjira river below the ramparts. The remains of the dome now lie fallen on the southern side of this building. This room resembles in its design and dimensions the tomb of Humayun Shah at Ashtur, suggesting that this palace dates from this sultan's short reign, or that his tomb sought to replicate the throne that he so courageously fought to attain.

From the throne room, visitors can now descend to the pool house (*c.* 1500) by returning to the lotus-pool courtyard, and taking the steps along its southern wall leading to a large rectangular open-air pool. Overlooking this pool is a recreational space divided by arches into three compartments decorated with elaborate stucco ornamentation. Additional octagonal pools clad in turquoise hexagonal tiles are situated at the ground-floor level of this building, but cannot be easily seen.

The palace where the *zenana* apartments, or women's quarters, were probably located also has a façade with a tripartite disposition: a *mandapa* with four columns framed by rectangular rooms. To the west is an octagonal space with large openings overlooking the lower garden. From here, steps lead to underground apartments probably used by the sultan and his private household as a cool retreat during the hot summer months.

Southwest of the *zenana* palace is an underground structure known as Hazar Kothri. Its impressive vaulted rooms do not betray the fact that from here the royal family could escape in an emergency to the triple ditch of the moat, and from there to the Bahmani army camp.

Palace III (Ladies Palace) – Octagonal room overlooking the lower garden, c. 1440

Water reservoir
with barrage and
sluices northwest
of palaces, c. 1430

Southeast of the Takht Mahal, to the north of the
Archaeological Museum, is a path that leads to the gardens below
the promontory, above which stands the *zenana* palace complex
just described. Here, an impressive gate separates the area where
horses and elephants were stabled from the lower royal garden. At
present, the lower royal garden is used by farmers who continue to
exploit the irrigation works established by the Bahmanis. If visitors
continue northwards, the large reservoir with its barrage and sluices
will appear. It is worth touring this area in the late afternoon, in
order to discover a number of *baolis* and enjoy a romantic view of
the Fort from the north.

Visitors may now return to the Gumbad Darwaza to see
the granaries started by Ahmad Shah. These are located on the
northern side of the gate, en route to the Mandu Darwaza in the
northeastern section of the ramparts. The granaries are among the
most interesting Bahmani buildings, as many of the engineering
and design innovations experimented here were later applied to
tombs and other structures. The granaries housed rice, millet, oil
and other commodities necessary for provisioning the fort and
city. In fact, it could be said that the true wealth of the region was
preserved in these structures, so that the court could satisfy the
fundamental needs of the citizens. Recent archaeological work
on the way to the granaries and along the ramparts has unearthed
several interconnecting water canals with small almond-shaped

lobed pools associated with a pavilion. Visitors may continue along this northwestern section of the Fort to reach the Mandu Darwaza. In one of the bastions here is a large canon dating from the reign of Ali Shah Baridi. This was once embellished with inlaid metallic motifs, as suggested by its carved recesses.

ASHTUR

The necropolis at Ashtur, 3 kilometres northeast of Bidar Fort, sits in a fertile plain that extends well beyond the city. Here are located the tombs of the Bahmani sultans as well as their spiritual advisors, the Nimatullahis. Approaching from Bidar Fort, visitors will notice tombs in the valleys on either side of the road, some of which predate the relocation of the Bahmani capital to Bidar. To the east of Ashtur there was once a lake and a barrage. Numerous *baolis* in the vicinity indicate that the area was once covered with gardens.

The tour of Ashtur commences with the Chaukhandi, or four-storeyed building, a dignified funerary complex that marks the last resting place of Shah Nimatullah's descendants. From here the eternal *baraka*, or blessing, of the spiritual preceptors of the late Bahmani sultans could flow outwards to bless the Fort and its rulers. Recently an enclosure wall has been built around this group of monuments. Beneath a tamarind tree is the tomb of a recent saint, and east of it an impressive restored *baoli* (*c.* 1450). To reach the top of the small hill where the Nimatullahi tombs are located, visitors must climb a number of steps to an insensitively restored gateway. On the southwest side of this gate is a two-storeyed structure, probably intended to accommodate pilgrims. Just before reaching the main

The Chaukhandi, containing the tomb of Khalilullah at Ashtur, c. 1458

Quranic inscriptions in the Chaukhandi, carved in basalt on the tomb of Khalilullah, c. 1458

mausoleum visitors will notice a small square anonymous tomb with a beautifully decorated stucco interior. The dome within displays a medallion design comprising concentric bands of foliate motifs; framing the four sides of the dome are stucco chains with overhanging medallions, with some traces of colouring.

The mausoleum of Hadrat Khalilullah (c. 1458) within the Chaukhandi dates from Alauddin Bahman II Shah's reign. Free-standing, double-tiered octagonal screen walls encase the small free-standing domed square tomb of the son of Shah Nimatullah. These were originally decorated with tilework, while the openings in the double-arched façade were outlined in grey-green basalt carved with bold, bevelled motifs. What is probably the finest example of Quranic calligraphy in the Deccan can be seen on the carved basalt panels above the southern entrance to the tomb. The elegant cursive script unfolds against a dynamic background of vegetal ornament. The interior corridor preceding the tomb is divided by arches into three domed bays, the central dome being lobed, on kite-shaped pendentives. To expand the space for the Nimatullahi burials, a domed square chamber was added to the southeastern face of the screen wall, and an open-air extension added to the western face. The tomb interior presents stucco designs on both its square exterior and octagonal interior. Perhaps its most interesting features are the small rooms occupying all

Tombs of the
Bahmani sultans,
east of the
Chaukhandi,
Ashtur, *c.* 1458

sides of the octagonal plan above ground-floor level, which can
be reached by steps. These were probably used for meditation by
murids of the saint or his descendants. Two additional tombs on the
northeastern side have wonderful stucco designs but are in a sorry
state of preservation.

Some 500 metres to the east of the Chaukhandi are the tombs
of the Bahmani sultans, as well as those of several of their wives
and children. These mausolea are precisely aligned on both sides
of a broad avenue: those of the kings on the north; those of other
family members on the south. The sole exception is a tomb believed
to be that of Ahmad Shah's wife, which stands below the platform
of her husband's mausoleum. The first and earliest mausoleum of
this group is that of Ahmad Shah at the eastern end of the platform
on which the royal tombs are aligned. This square, massively built
edifice has its façades decorated with arched recesses at different
scales. The central and largest arch is embellished with stucco
roundels, while that on the northern gate is inscribed with the
Throne Verse from the Quran. However, it is the interior that is the
glory of this tomb. This is embellished with splendid paintings, the
most complete example of mural art in any Islamic edifice in the
Deccan. The murals are both accomplished and innovative, since
they combine local Deccani- as well as Timurid-derived traditions
in order to express Ahmad Shah's ecumenical spirituality as well as

Painted squinches and walls of the tomb of Ahmad Shah Wali, 1436

his artistic cosmopolitanism. Different themes decorate the walls, the zone of transition beneath the dome, and the dome itself. The lower part of the wall, though repainted numerous times, imitates designs in hexagonal and triangular tilework. A white band above is inscribed with a tract by Shah Nimatullah. Above the windows are beautifully executed oak- or lotus-leaf motifs with emerging flower bouquets. Cloud-collar compositions in black and eight-pointed medallions in bluish-grey adorn vibrant red bands around the windows, while the arches display bands with star-shaped designs. Depictions of vases holding tree shapes fill the spaces between the squinches, which in turn are decorated with inscriptions and geometric designs. The dome itself is embellished with a magnificent, bold design of hanging ornaments; in its centre are concentric bands of inscriptions pertaining to Shah Nimatullah's spiritual associations. Blessings are inscribed on white bands surmounting all the openings, together with historical inscriptions informing the visitor that the affairs of state were entrusted to Ahmad Shah in 1422, and that "He lived in the world to be praised and returned to his God to be blessed on the night of 29 Ramadan 839" (that is, 17 April 1436). The painted decor is signed by Shukrullah of Qazwin, evidently a master artist. A particularly unusual feature of the painted decor is the allegorical depiction of paradise in the *mihrab*. Here, a scalloped blind covered in elegant arabesque designs in brown, white and rust reveals the golden light of paradise, as implied by the verses inscribed above the *mihrab* (unfortunately now damaged).

To the south and below Ahmad Shah's tomb is probably the tomb of one of his four sons. On the interior walls of this tomb, one can admire some of the finest stucco designs of the Bahmani period consisting of inscriptions, lotus and other foliate motifs.

Next to Ahmad Shah's tomb is a recently built mosque. Beyond is the mausoleum of Alauddin Ahmad II (d. 1458), Ahmad Shah's son and successor. The tomb is of interest architecturally since it introduces several unusual innovations. Its façades are no longer divided into superimposed tiers of arched niches; instead, the niches follow a descending order on both sides of the central highest arches that mark the entrances on three sides as well as the location of the *mihrab* within. Together with the squares, rectangles, lozenges and bands below leaf-shaped merlons, these niches are outlined by basalt rods of different designs, some with

Polychrome underglaze painted tiles on the tomb of Alauddin Ahmad Shah, c. 1458

exquisitely bevelled foliate and geometric ornament. On the southern façade of the tomb, the two decorative bands below the merlons are embellished with Kufic and cursive inscriptions in polychrome mosaic tilework. Indeed, it is only this southern façade that seems to have been decorated. The underglaze-painted tiles depict foliate and calligraphic themes, as well as lotus petals and oak leaves with flowers. The tomb's interior is also unique, since the zones around its windows are distinguished by deep recesses that could accommodate praying visitors.

The tomb of Humayun Shah (d. 1461), Alauddin's son is located next to that of his father. Its dome must have been one of the loftiest in Ashtur, but has since fallen. The tomb interior has deep square recesses in its walls; steps on its eastern side lead to the roof. The *mihrab* follows a five-sided configuration, as do the *mihrabs* within the tombs of his successors, Ahmad Shah (d. 1463) and Muhammad III (d. 1482), both left unfinished. The *mihrab* of Muhammad III's tomb has its sides marked by recessed arched niches and outlined with intersecting plaster bands that form a fan-shaped, star-like dome.

Opposite the tombs of the sultans is that of Makhduma-i-Jahan Nargis Begum, Mistress of the World, the wife of Humayun Shah and mother of his two successors. Upon the death of Humayun in 1461, she was regent in a triumvirate that ruled the Bahmani kingdom for a number of years with the help of Mahmud

The interior of the tomb of Mahmud Shah, c. 1482

Gawan, until her own death in 1472. Her tomb is smaller than those of her husband and children, while its decorative scheme adheres to that of the early Bahmani tombs, in which stucco designs predominate. The *mihrab* of her tomb is also unusual, as it is long and narrow, and follows a three-lobed design.

The tomb of Mahmud Shah (d. 1518) is the last grandiose mausoleum at Ashtur. Ironically, it was erected for a ruler whose power was only nominal. It is located between the incomplete tomb of Muhammad III, already described, and the diminutive funerary monument of one of the last Bahmanis, Ahmad Shah IV (d.1520). Its façades display three tiers of arched niches, elegantly outlined in stucco or basalt. Separating these tiers are stucco bands imitating a rope, a design that was to become one of the favoured decorative themes of the Adil Shahis. The southern gate entrance is marked by a square imitation temple stone with a circle in relief. The merlons are also in two tiers, the upper one surrounding the octagon of the dome embracing elaborate *guldastas*. The interior walls of Mahmud III's tomb are also divided into arched tiers, with intersecting plaster bands. The niches on the surface of the squinches are framed by intersecting bands in plaster, a design that is also repeated on the faceted mihrab. The octagonal drum is decorated with niches, above which are merlons with the customary guldastas.

The tombs, including that of Shah Rukh Khan, near Ashtur, c. 1500

The next four mausolea at Ashtur, one of them ruined, belonged to the last Bahmani rulers, who were hostages of the powerful and ambitious minister, Amir I Baridi. Two of these are situated to the south and two to the west of Mahmud Shah's tomb. The incomplete mausoleum on the south side could belong to Alauddin Shah (d. 1521) and the one next to it to his brother, Ahmad Shah IV (d. 1521). Those to the west commemorate the last Bahmani sultans, Wallilullah (d. 1526) and Kalimullah (d. 1538). The tombs are all small and square and are roofed not by domes but by pyramidal vaults, indicating perhaps that by the time they were built these figures no longer enjoyed royal privilege. Despite their small size, the three tombs repeat features of their predecessors, and introduce new schemes, such as the deep domed corner spaces with intersecting arches.

One of the most interesting tombs at Ashtur is that of Shah Rukh Khan (c.1500), overlooking the royal necropolis from a hill located to the north of Mahmud Shah's mausoleum and to the nearby village. Close to it is one more tomb. The smaller tomb contains an impressive basalt cenotaph, while Rukh Khans' tomb,

Detail of stucco decoration on tomb of Shah Rukh Khan

Interior of the tomb
of Shah Rukh Khan

housing two burials, is decorated with artfully executed stucco designs. These comprise chains with overhanging ornaments within lobed panels, the Throne Verse (Quran ii, 256) over the eastern doorway and a profusion of vegetal motifs.

NIMATABAD

For visitors with additional time and interest, there are a number of ruined settlements dating from Bahmani times in the vicinity of Bidar. Some 6 kilometres northwest of Ashtur is the resort of Nimatabad, where the Bahmani sultans would escape the formalities of the court. Nimatabad was granted to the descendants of Shah Nimatullah by Ahmad Shah. Its location is tranquil and pleasant, as it occupies a promontory overlooking the Manjira river.

Tomb of Fakhr al-Mulk on the way to Nimatabad, c. 1500

Along the banks are a number of *baolis*; in the fields nearby are the remains of impressive walls with embedded pink granite columns with arches and niches.

En route to Nimatabad, on an elevation surrounded by steep steps which resemble those of local bathing ghats, is the tomb of Fakhr al-Mulk (*c.* 1500). At the summit of the hill, the area around the tomb is enclosed by thick walls. The sepulchre here is situated in the middle of a square and shallow water basin, indicating that during the monsoons or heavy rains pilgrims would have had to wade through the water in order to reach the mausoleum's gate. The tomb itself is in two parts, the more interesting being the basement where the cenotaph of this presumed Bahmani dignitary is sheltered beneath an octagonal pyramidal vault that imitates a tent. An opening on the northern wall at ground level leads to steps and to a corridor around the dome, from which magnificent views of the surrounding area can be enjoyed.

SOUTH OF BIDAR

The approach to Bidar, along the road from Hyderabad, reveals in the distance the domes of the most important Chishti shrine of the city, that of Shah Abu'l Faid (d. 1474), a contemporary of no less than four Bahmani sultans. The saint's tomb sits within a large walled enclosure, probably built during Muhammad Shah III's reign. Layers of whitewash have almost obliterated the external plasterwork of the structure, while many of the underglaze-painted tiles that framed its entrance have been replaced by painted imitations. The interior plaster decoration of the tomb has also been subjected to coats of over-painting, in which a pink colour has been freely used. Below the dome are the graves of the saint and two of his relatives; graves of other relations are located in front and in the vaulted space west of this tomb. Of particular interest is the music hall located south of the tomb. Here *qawwalis* (Sufi devotional music) are still performed by dervishes on special occasions.

KAMTHANA

Some 10 kilometres southwest of Bidar, visitors will pass by an arch, which is the only remaining vestige of the Bahmani suburb of Kamthana. Nearby is an 11th-century reservoir and embankment, with several sluices controlling the flow of water to the nearby arable lands. During the Bahmani and Baridi periods, this embankment was repaired several times, and was linked by a *qanat* to a water tank. It is probable that the tank was located in the middle of a garden, as is suggested by an abundance of mango and tamarind trees that can still be seen in the vicinity.

WEST OF BIDAR

The tombs and polo ground of the Baridis, some 2 kilometres west of Bidar Fort, are easily reached by following the road that leads to Humnabad. The first structure to be built on this side of the city was the tomb of Qasim Baridi I (d. 1504). Although insignificant architecturally, this mausoleum belongs to the founder of the dynasty. Qasim Baridi I never assumed a royal title, remaining a minister of the puppet Bahmani ruler, Mahmud Shah. The tomb is a small, square mausoleum with a pyramidal vault located next to the larger, but incomplete, tomb of his son, Amir Baridi I (d.1543).

The tomb of Amir Baridi's brother, Khan Jahan (*c.* 1550), is raised on a high platform and sits at the midpoint of a formal square space. This space is defined by a narrow water channel carved into the laterite clay and fed from the outside by a well. The square outline of the water body is repeated twice by two sets of orthogonal paths that become narrower as the visitor approaches the platform of the tomb, from which radiate additional paths. At the intersections of these framing squares and paths sit small octagonal platforms. Outside the square water body, at the southwest corner of this planned landscape, are a mosque, a residential building for visitors to the tomb and a square pool served by an adjoining *baoli*. This complex is the first Deccani example of a tomb placed in the middle of a symmetrical, cross-axial garden.

The orthogonal layout of this landscape is repeated in the majestic tomb of Ali Shah Baridi, which this sultan completed three years before his death in 1580. Ali was the first Baridi ruler to adopt the title Shah, and his regal status is reflected in the monumental scale of his tomb. The mausoleum, raised on a lofty platform, imitates the plan of a garden pavilion. It has four majestic arches, framed on both sides by double tiers of arched niches, above

which are four decorative bands followed by leaf merlons and corner *guldastas*. The composition is crowned by an onion-shaped dome. Beneath the dome is the sultan's beautifully carved basalt cenotaph. This is inscribed with the Islamic creed, together with dates marking the completion of the monument and the king's death. The tomb's interior is decorated with polychrome tiled panels set within basalt frames. The panels are filled with monumental thuluth script worthy of the Quran; they also contain verses from the Persian poet Attar, as well as the name of the calligraphist Khwajagi from Shirwan, in the eastern Caucasus.

A humbler copy of Ali Baridi Shah's tomb is represented by that of his son Ibrahim (d. 1587), which abuts the western enclosure wall of his

Tomb of Khan Jahan, c. 1550

father's funerary enclosure. Here, engaged octagonal columns embellishing the arched openings were probably inspired by those of the tombs at Ashtur, already described. Ibrahim Baridi's tomb is entered from the south via an impressive gate that also served as a residential building. On the southwest side of this tomb and its garden, outside its walls, is a complex comprising a square pool, mosque and residential structure. Between the residential structure and pool is a small symmetrical garden with *baolis* and fountains.

To the north of Ali Baridi's tomb was the polo ground of the Bahmanis and Baridis. Four heavy pink-granite pillars, partly concealed now by piles of rubbish, are the only indicators of the

The tomb of
Ali Shah Baridi
imitates the plan
of a grand pavilion,
c. 1580

field where one of the most popular games of the Deccani sultans took place. The funerary complex of Qasim II Baridi (d. 1591) was once surrounded by an enclosed garden entered through a gate, the only reminder of which are some neglected mango trees. Southwest of this tomb is a square pool that was probably fed by a well located outside the enclosure; due south of the pool is a mosque. This tomb and the unidentified other tombs with which it is closely associated have been restored, and the surrounding area converted into a popular park.

BIJAPUR

PRECEDING PAGES:
Jami Masjid mihrab,
Bijapur, 1636

Bijapur was an important stronghold of the Khaljis and Tughluqs until 1347 when it became the seat of a local governor under the Bahmanis; it was given to Mahmud Gawan by Humayun Shah after the latter's accession to the throne in 1458. Mahmud Gawan was succeeded in this province by Yusuf Adil Khan, his adopted son who, in 1490, declared his independence from the Bahmani sultan

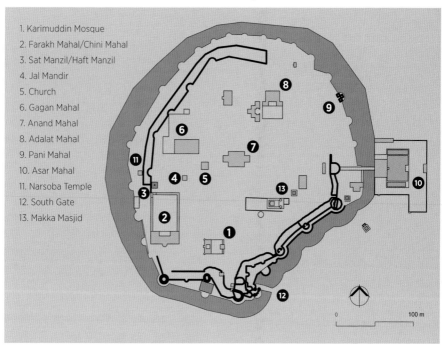

1. Karimuddin Mosque
2. Farakh Mahal/Chini Mahal
3. Sat Manzil/Haft Manzil
4. Jal Mandir
5. Church
6. Gagan Mahal
7. Anand Mahal
8. Adalat Mahal
9. Pani Mahal
10. Asar Mahal
11. Narsoba Temple
12. South Gate
13. Makka Masjid

0   100 m

Bijapur citadel Ark
Qila

in Bidar. Yusuf Adil Khan's successor, Ibrahim I, in turn, assumed the title of "Shah" in 1538.

For over 150 years, Bijapur flourished as the capital of the Adil Shahi line of rulers presiding over a wealthy and influential kingdom. Perhaps more than any other Deccani rulers of the era, the sultans and queens of Bijapur sponsored a magnificent, highly individual style of architecture that is reflected in both their religious and courtly buildings. Their patronage extended to literature and the arts, transforming Bijapur into the preeminent intellectual and artistic centre of the Deccan, rivalling in splendour that of the contemporary Mughal capitals of Northern India.

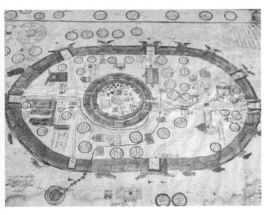

Map of Bijapur, 17th century, Archaeological Museum, Gol Gumbaz

Bijapur retains much of its original Adil Shahi layout and monuments. The fortifications and moats, though incompletely preserved, define an irregular oval-shaped plan some 3 kilometres along its major east-west axis, slightly less along its north-south axis. Within the ramparts stand a large number of religious, courtly and ceremonial structures, together with *baolis* and other hydraulic features that supplied water to the city during the 16th and 17th centuries. In recent years, Bijapur's historical buildings have become increasingly obscured by modern dwellings, and almost nothing now remains of the luxuriant gardens with which Bijapur was once endowed.

Situated centrally within the city walls is a circular zone with its own, independent ring of walls and a moat. This is the citadel, or Ark Qila, the centre of the kingdom and its capital, where the Adil Shahi rulers and their court resided. Here can be seen numerous audience halls, residential palaces and pleasure pavilions. Other royal monuments are located outside the city walls, in the suburbs and resorts that were founded during the 16th and 17th centuries.

To facilitate the visit of Bijapur's rich array of historical monuments, the tour described here is divided into a number of urban zones. It begins with the citadel at the core of the walled city and then proceeds in an anticlockwise direction through the four quadrants of Bijapur. Only then are the monuments in the suburbs and resorts outside the walled city described.

THE CITADEL

Originally surrounded by a moated fortified enclosure, Bijapur's Ark Qila, or citadel, accommodated the principal Adil Shahi administrative and residential headquarters. The stone revetments were added to the earlier Bahmani earthen walls by Yusuf Adil Khan in the early-16th century. They were augmented by his successors over a period of more than 40 years, as indicated by inscriptions on the blocks embedded in the citadel walls.

Two storeyed
transverse hall,
Chini Mahal, 1514
and later. Presently
an administrative
office

The only surviving gateway to the citadel is the South
Gate. This continued to be remodelled, at least until the Mughal
occupation, in response to military innovations. The gate is
protected by an angled entryway, which crosses a barbican, followed
by the outer walls, which are separated from the South Gate by a
courtyard that probably dates from the 16th and 17th centuries;
beyond it, on the western side of a further courtyard, are earlier
walls that most likely belong to the 15th-century Bahmani period.
This second courtyard is Adil Shahi, and was probably meant for
the citadel's guards. From here visitors may glimpse several free-
standing temple columns.

Immediately inside this South Gate stands Karimuddin's
Mosque, the earliest Islamic monument in Bijapur. This was built
in 1320 on the site of a Hindu temple, the entrance porch of which
survives; the mosque's interior employs reused temple columns,
beams and ceiling slabs throughout. Karimuddin, the son of Malik
Kafur, who headed the invading Delhi army of the Khalji sultan,
was responsible for several successful campaigns against the Hindu
kingdoms in the Deccan. This mosque must have served as the *Jami
Masjid* of Bijapur until the end of the 16th century, when Ali I Adil
Shah erected his own congregational mosque (described below).
Most probably Karimuddin's Mosque was where Yusuf Adil Khan

View of ornamental
pool of the Haft
Manzil, or Sat
Manzil, 1590

would have read the Friday sermon; it might even have been the place where he introduced the Shi'a faith to the Deccan.

Historical chroniclers of Bijapur list at least ten royal palaces and pavilions inside the Ark Qila. Of these, some were later destroyed and others fell into ruin; others were in more recent times remodelled as offices or accommodation for state dignitaries. It is not clear how these palaces and pavilions related to each other in the ceremonial life of the Adil Shahis, except that they followed an overall north-south alignment. The royal edifices stress verticality in their architectural treatment and are all multi-storeyed, flat-roofed structures with monumental tripartite façades. Behind each façade of these structures was a raised portico preceded by timber or rubble-stone columns that framed an elevated loggia, the entire composition being originally reflected in a pool. The interiors of some palaces used timber, while the better-preserved ones are of stone.

Southwest of Karimuddin's Mosque is the Farakh Mahal, the oldest surviving ceremonial structure of the Adil Shahis, better known today as the Chini Mahal. Of its tripartite arched façade, nothing survives, except the footing blocks of the columns that formed its portico. The broad two-storeyed hall that runs parallel to this façade has four pointed arches that divide its interior into three

Vault with fine
plaster decorations
in Haft Manzil, 1590

bays, each roofed with a dome. On the building's western and eastern corners are balconies; its central area opens into a room with a polygonal apse that may have served as a reception hall for private audiences and is now an office. Above this section of the palace was the ceremonial loggia of the sultan, covered by a small dome on pendentives and reached by steps that are now blocked by metal cupboards. Further steps located in the western section of the palace ascend to more spacious arched halls on the upper floor.

The courtyard with pool, which probably once preceded the arched façade of the Chini Mahal, is now occupied by buildings that form a rectangle around an open court, replacing earlier royal structures. At the northwestern corner of this court is the Haft Manzil, or Sat Manzil (Seven Pavilions), built by Ibrahim II in 1590. It overlooks what remains of the fort's moat and the Narsoba temple. The Haft Manzil is a private multi-storeyed pavilion, with ornamental pools and fountains set into the floors on each of its ascending, receding levels. The internal vaulting displays fine plaster decoration, some of it imitating timber construction. Virtually nothing survives of the wall paintings, which, according to 19th-century descriptions, depicted courtly figures engaged in pleasurable pursuits. The Adil Shahi rulers had a predilection for high buildings, in which the ruler would appear as if floating under the firmament, and this multi-storeyed structure fulfilled this function.

From its northern face the Haft Manzil overlooks a small basalt pavilion, exquisitely decorated with hanging ornaments and brackets that support balconies, crowned by a dome on lotus-petal

The Jal Mandir, or Water Pavilion, crowned by a dome on lotus-petal motifs, early 17th century

motifs. Known as the Jal Mandir, or Water Pavilion, this early-17th-century structure is set within a square pool. However, it cannot be reached, nor is its single chamber large enough for any visitor. Quite possibly it was originally intended as a reliquary for the two hairs from the Prophet's beard acquired by Ibrahim II, later accommodated in the Asar Mahal (described below).

The Gagan Mahal, or Heavenly Palace, built by Ali I, 1558–80

Continuing north, visitors will encounter a small gateway now used as a church. This square masonry structure has carved stones embedded in its walls: some depict lions; others are inscribed. This was probably the gateway to the group of palaces on the northern side of the citadel, which the visitor is now approaching.

The Gagan Mahal, or Heavenly Palace, was built by Ali I after the battle of Talikota in 1565 as part of his transformation of Bijapur into the capital of a newly powerful kingdom. Only the masonry shell of this imposing ceremonial edifice survives; its timber interiors have disappeared. Its majestic, tall, broad central arch is framed by narrower arches and decorated with carved plaster designs of fish-like brackets supporting roundels carved with vegetal themes. The royal loggia located under the apex of its arch symbolised the ruler's role as divine mediator. Other domed loggias with balconies on the upper levels, reached by steep steps, were probably used by the ruler on different ceremonial occasions.

A few metres east of the Gagan Mahal is the Anand Mahal, or Palace of Pleasure, constructed by Ibrahim II in 1591. During the early-20th century this was converted into municipal offices and a sports-recreation club. On both sides of the main, broad four-storeyed façade are extensions. On the ground floor, some plaster designs on the vaults imitate timber structures.

| 114

Anand Mahal, or Palace of Pleasure, now municipal offices and a sports-recreation club, 1591

In the northeast section of the citadel, within the present-day private garden of a government official, is the elegant Pani Mahal, or Water Palace, of 1671. This overlooked the moat that once surrounded the Ark Qila and, beyond it to the east, the Asar Mahal. In the southeastern section of the citadel stands Makka Masjid, added in the 17th century. Concealed behind high walls, this mosque has two minarets on its eastern side that must have belonged to an earlier structure. That this mosque was decorated by the best artists of the kingdom is demonstrated by its *mihrab*, which is embellished with niches, hanging ornaments and depictions of miniature edifices.

Pani Mahal, or Water Palace, 1671

A footbridge carried on a broad, low arch spanning the moat once connected the palaces within the citadel to the Asar Mahal situated immediately outside its eastern walls. This audience hall was erected in 1646 during the reign of Muhammad Adil Shah. The footbridge was connected by paths leading from the several bastions of the citadel to its various levels, permitting the sultan to gain direct access from different areas of the fort. Set within a walled garden, the Asar Mahal was originally intended as a hall of public audience, but within just a few years, it was converted into a religious building that accommodated the holy relic of the Prophet, which may have been housed previously in the Jal Mandir. The palace followed an east-west orientation, and instead of the customary masonry tripartite façade, timber columns were used to create a lofty verandah, at the rear of which was a throne loggia raised on a platform with arched openings. Only the elite of the kingdom had access to this upper floor and loggia where some of the palace's most beautifully decorated rooms are located. (Only male visitors are admitted today.) These rooms are adorned with different painted themes, including vases with flowers and bejewelled, voluptuous courtly ladies. The façade of the Asar Mahal is mirrored in the three pools that occupy the garden to the east. The northern entrance to this garden was originally via the Jahaz Mahal, or Ship Palace. In this impressive, but now derelict, building the admiralty was housed; it is possible that the considerable Adil Shahi commercial fleet was controlled from here.

Detail of *mihrab* embellished with niches, hanging ornaments and depictions of miniature edifices in Makka Masjid, 17th century

Asar Mahal, the northern entrance to the compound is through the Jahaz Mahal or Ship Palace, 1646

NORTHEAST ZONE

This part of Bijapur is dominated by the tomb of Muhammad Adil Shah (d. 1656), known popularly as the Gol Gumbad, or Round Dome. This majestic edifice is set within a large compound of gardens, *baolis* and water towers situated near the fortification walls

Painted vase in
niche of Asar
Mahal, 1646

in the northeast quadrant of the city. The tomb was left unfinished
at Muhammad's death, when the plastering of the walls and other
final touches were still in progress. While the mausoleum of his
father, the Ibrahim Rauza, was an elegant, poetic tribute to the
composite cultures of the Deccan, the Gol Gumbad broke past
tradition by introducing a grand vision of majesty to the region.

In order to best appreciate this extraordinary monument, visitors should first see it from a distance so as to gain an appreciation of its huge scale and purity of line. Like the tomb itself, the two-storeyed *naqqar khana*, or drum house, that precedes it was never completed; the brackets at the top of its façades were supposed to carry an overhanging cornice followed by a parapet, the whole building being framed by two minarets. At present the *naqqar khana* is occupied by the Archaeological Museum. Among the remarkable objects in its collection is an inscribed sandstone column dated to the early-7th century removed from the Hindu pilgrimage site of Mahakuta, near Badami. Here, too, are displayed several elegantly inscribed calligraphic blocks, as well as a wooden statue of an Adil Shahi sultan that was probably taken around the city in procession, like the metal images of Hindu gods that were borne aloft during special ceremonies. In the museum's upper level is a 17th-century watercolour map of Bijapur, depicting the oval-shaped ramparts, and with labels identifying the city's principal gateways, palaces, mosques, tombs and waterworks. There are also several splendid, though worn, carpets, metal objects and Chinese ceramics that were

Gol Gumbad, the tomb of Muhammad Adil Shah, *c.* 1656

found in the palace area of the citadel.

Between the Gol Gumbad and the *naqqar khana* is a pool for ritual ablutions, behind which rises the immense southern façade of the tomb itself. Its hemispherical dome, which measures nearly 44 metres in external diameter, surrounded by lotus leaves, cannot be seen from this point, but a circumambulation will permit a better appreciation of the monument's immense scale. Triple-arched niches covered in stucco occupy three façades; the central sections are filled with a basalt screen of cut-out "gateways" and arched windows. The typical Adil Shahi motif of a bracket supporting a roundel adorns the corner niches; the apexes of the arched niches display banana-bud emblems against wing-shaped foliation. Running atop the façades is a basalt cornice supported on carved brackets projecting well away from the wall. Above the cornice are arched openings topped by merlons with four *guldastas* on each face. The juxtaposition of basalt and stucco adds a colourful effect to this otherwise sober structure, as do the octagonal corner towers with seven stages of open windows lighting interior staircases, topped by bulbous domes. Unlike the pool on the south side of the Gol Gumbad, those on the other three sides are merely ornamental basins.

Within the tomb, over the southern entrance, is a Persian inscription in three parts; the values of the letters in the words yield a date equivalent to 1656, the year of the sultan's death. The austerity of the Gol Gumbad's interior draws attention to the structural virtuosity of its unknown architect. Eight lofty intersecting arches create interlocking pendentives that support the huge dome that dominates the space. The dome is constructed of corbelled rings of bricks set in high-quality mortar, with the thickness of the structural shell reducing gradually as the dome rises. Under this vast airy space, lies the cenotaph slab of Muhammad. The actual tombs of the ruler, his mother and other relatives, however, are situated in a ground-level crypt, now inaccessible to visitors. A staircase within the thickness of the walls ascends to the gallery at the base of the dome, famous for its remarkable echoes. At each landing, there are small spaces for visitors or attendants to rest or meditate.

To the west of the tombs is the attendant mosque, with its modest five-arched façade and pair of attached minarets. In the past this served as a travellers' bungalow, which perhaps explains its current poor condition.

NORTHWEST ZONE

The itinerary of this part of Bijapur begins with the unfinished tomb of Ali II Adil Shah (d. 1672), the last royal mausoleum to be

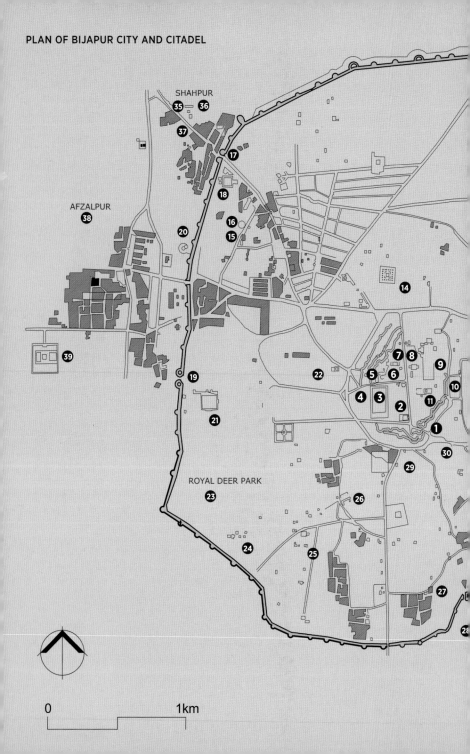

PLAN OF BIJAPUR CITY AND CITADEL

SHAHPUR

AFZALPUR

ROYAL DEER PARK

0   1km

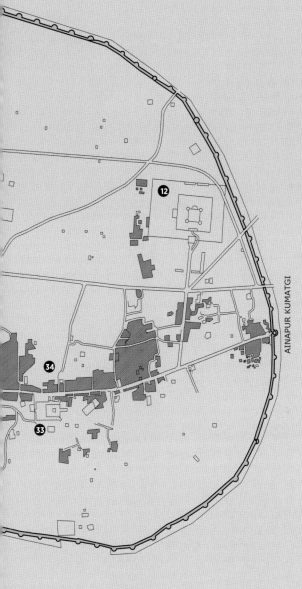

AINAPUR KUMATGI

1. South Darwaza
2. Karimuddin's Mosque
3. Chini Mahal
4. Haft Manzil
5. Jal mandir
6. Church
7. Gagan Mahal
8. Anand Mahal
9. Pani Mahal
10. Asar Mahal
11. Makka Masjid
12. Gol Gumbad
13. Rangini Masjid
14. Tomb of Ali II Adil Shah
15. *Idgah*
16. Haidar Burj
17. Shahpur Darwaza
18. Chand Baoli
19. Makka Darwaza
20. Sharza Burj and Malik-i-Maidan
    Mosque cannon
21. Taj Baoli
22. Malika Jahan Begum Mosque
23. Gumat Baoli
24. Tombs of Shaikh Hamid Qadiri
    and Latifullah Qadiri
25. Tomb of Ali I Adil Shah
26. Ibrahim's Old Mosque
27. Ikhlas Khan Mosque
28. Fath Darwaza
29. Anda Masjid
30. Mihtar Mahal
31. Asen Beg Mosque
32. Ali Shahid Pir's Mosque
33. *Jami Masjid*
34. Nau Gumbad
35. Hauz-i-Shahpur
36. *Sarai*
37. Chishti *Dargah*
38. Afzalpur
39. Ibrahim Rauza

The unfinished tomb of Ali II Adil Shah in the northwest zone of Bijapur, *c.* 1672

built in the city. The 16-year reign of this sultan was constantly threatened by Mughal attempts to conquer the Deccan. By 1686, Bijapur was annexed to the Mughal empire, and Ali II's tomb represents the end of Adil Shahi sovereignty. The mausoleum is raised on an elevated basement that supports a line of unfinished, cascading black-basalt arches, lending an air of grandeur to the unfinished mausoleum. The tombstone within is plain, while the adjacent mosque may have been an afterthought. The somewhat rough finish of the masonry suggests that the building would have been completed in plaster.

The next feature to be described here is the monumental *idgah* of 1538. This stands within the city walls, but at a location that at this time would have been outside the inhabited urban area. The *idgah* comprises a platform that ends in an immense sloping *qibla* wall. This is framed by two turrets with rooms at the top, covered with domes linked by a terrace. On these turrets are three arched balconies on brackets. The imposing *minbar* adjoining the deep *mihrab* is covered by a dome that projects on the eastern side of the wall. Monumental *idgahs*, such as this example, were not only used for important religious festivals, but were also the focus of royal ceremonies, during which the *minbar* served as the ruler's throne.

From the *idgah*, it is a short distance to the Haidar Burj, which rises amidst the busy streets and occupies the highest ground in the city, hence its popular appellation, "Upri" or "Upli", meaning "High"

The Chand Baoli surrounded by walls with arched niches, c. 1580

or "Lofty". This free-standing structure was built in 1583, probably to accommodate the longest iron cannon in Bijapur, which was too large for the normal towers on the fort walls. Not far from Haidar Burj is Chand Baoli, one of the most impressive water sources in Bijapur. The walls around the pool of Chand Baoli are decorated with arched niches with rectangular openings; on its southern and northern sides are habitable quarters, the most important of which is a two-storeyed pavilion with a triple-arched façade facing the pool from the north. As in the past, the areas closest to the water remain cool even in the hot season, and it is here that people gather while waiting for the relief of the monsoon rains.

Adjoining the Chand Baoli is the Shahpur Darwaza, one of the five principal entryways in the outer ring of Bijapur's city walls. The oldest inscription on its inner face is dated 1570–71, during the reign of Ali I. It was this sultan who established Shahpur, the residential suburb located outside this gate to the north of the city (described below).

SOUTHWEST ZONE

Visitors should now re-enter the city via the Makka Darwaza, the gateway erected by Malik Sandal in 1655–56. He was a general in the Adil Shahi army and a trusted servant of Taj Sultana, the surviving queen of Ibrahim II. The original Makka Darwaza was further fortified over the centuries to become an elaborate, impressive stronghold. Embedded in the gate's external wall is a stone carving of a two-bodied lion head, seizing with its paws an elephant, symbolising Bijapur's ambitions over its enemies.

Midway between the Makka and Shahpur Darwazas is Sharza Burj, or Lion Bastion. This was raised to receive the most famous cannon of the Deccan, known as the Malik-i-Maidan, or Lord of the Plain. Cast in a special alloy, the cannon was manufactured to fire not just cannon balls, but also metal slugs and even copper

The Makka Darwaza erected by Malik Sandal, 1655–6

coins, with which the defenders hoped to bribe the soldiers of invading armies. Its muzzle is fashioned into the head of a lion holding small elephants in its savage teeth. The maker of this remarkable weapon was Muhammad, son of Hasan Rumi, an immigrant from Anatolia (a region known at the time as Rum in present day Turkey); a date equivalent to 1549 is inscribed on its shaft. The cannon was originally manufactured for the Nizam Shahis of Ahmadnagar, and transported to the battle against Vijayanagara at Talikota where it played a major role, probably due more to its frightening noise than to its actual military value. It was subsequently brought to Bijapur in 1632 as a war trophy.

Carved lion motifs on the Sharza Burj

A short distance from the Makka Darwaza is the celebrated Taj Baoli built by Malik Sandal in the 17th century. To the north of this *baoli* once ran one of the main thoroughfares of the city; to the south lay the royal deer park. The Taj Baoli comprises a huge, rectangular step-well carved out of bedrock and enclosed by high stone walls on three sides. Apartments for travellers and visitors are located on the western and eastern sections of its northern side, where the entrance to the *baoli* is located, with a *hammam* on the northwestern side of this entrance. The wide entryway is framed by polygonal domed towers that open on to a broad pointed arch, below which are the steps descending to the water.

To the east of the Taj Baoli, approximately on axis with the Ibrahim Rauza outside the city walls, is the mosque of Malika Jahan Begum, popularly known as Zanjiri, because of its stone chain ornamentation (since disappeared). Attributed to Ibrahim II's reign, this mosque is an architectural gem, and boasts some of the most exquisitely carved decoration to be seen in any of Bijapur's buildings.

From the mosque of Malika Jahan Begum it is but a short distance to the tombs of Sheikh Hamid Qadiri (d. 1602) and Latifullah Qadiri (d. 1612), with their associated mosque. Nearby is the Gumat Baoli built by Fatima Sultana in 1562, located near the enclosure walls in this quadrant of the city. Some 400 metres northeast of the Qadiri tomb is the mausoleum of Ali I Adil Shah (d. 1580), the first royal mausoleum to be erected in Bijapur. (Ali

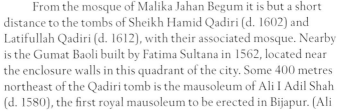

Malik-i-Maidan, or Lord of the Plain, the most impressive cannon of the Deccan that fired cannon balls, metal slugs and copper coins, 1549

I's predecessors were all buried in the *dargah* of Hazrat Chand Husayni at Gogi, about 115 kilometres east of the city.) Ali's tomb is a modest but well-proportioned square structure located within a now-abandoned fenced garden enclosure. The sepulchral chamber, with its five anonymous cenotaphs, is surrounded by a corridor covered with a vault on all four sides, and an arcade consisting of two large side arches framing three smaller arches. The chamber's exterior walls were once painted with geometric patterns and inscriptions mentioning Allah, Muhammad and the Shi'a profession of faith. The chamber is divided internally by transverse arches into three bays roofed with domes on kite-shaped pendentives. On the northern side of the tomb is an open-air burial platform built for Prince Daulat Afza (d.1688), grandson of Emperor Aurangzeb. This magnificent and beautifully carved dolerite construction is unequalled in Bijapur. It comprises a large platform in the shape of an opulent footstool, on which stands a male stone

Taj Baoli, 17th century

Tomb of Ali I Adil Shah, c. 1580

125

cenotaph, possibly belonging to a relative of the king or some other nobleman. Steps located on the northern section of the platform lead to the burial chamber below.

The so-called Ibrahim's Old *Jami Masjid* is situated a short distance northeast of Ali I's tomb. The mosque, which is a 16th-century construction, is a triple-bay structure with receding arches. A *chhajja* on brackets and pendant lotus motifs shade these arches; rising from the corner piers are large polygonal domed pinnacles. Domes must also have topped the two polygonal minarets that rise above the central piers of the façade; their square bases with arched niches support polygonal shafts also decorated with bands of arched niches.

Closely resembling this early mosque is the contemporary Ikhlas Khan Mosque located near the Fath Darwaza. A significant difference to Ibrahim's Old Jami is the rooftop pavilion with a deep dome on kite-shaped pendentives above its *mihrab*. The only known historical figure named Ikhlas Khan was a Habshi nobleman responsible for Ibrahim II's education, but whether it was this figure who actually built the mosque is not known.

SOUTHEAST ZONE

The first monument of interest to be described in this part of Bijapur is the Anda Masjid. This unusual two-storeyed mosque has a congregational hall on its ground floor and a prayer hall with a *minbar* on the upper level. The prayer hall has a triple-arched façade opening onto a large verandah. This is sheltered by an overhanging *chhajja* on stone brackets; from the corners of the building rise two polygonal minarets with balconies and ribbed bulbous domes. Similar minarets are seen at the corners of the hall's western façade; four more minarets of the same type punctuate the corners of the protruding *mihrab*. The minarets are linked by a carved parapet. The hall's interior decoration, comprising foliate and other motifs, is amongst the most refined in Bijapur. The historical inscription around the entrance door informs visitors that this mosque was built in 1608 by Itibar Khan, a nobleman in the service of Ibrahim II and Muhammad Adil Shah.

Not far from the Anda Masjid is the Mihtar Mahal (*c.* 1620). This comprises a multi-storeyed gatehouse, framed by slender corner minarets, that opens on its western side onto a mosque courtyard. The Mihtar Mahal is a showpiece of the most refined carving. Among its decorative themes are lions, geese, foliate designs and geometric motifs. Its overhanging balconies, carried on angled, perforated brackets, suggest timber originals. The lowest level of its façade presents an arched doorway with recessed planes set within a masterfully built masonry wall, the stones of which are carved with cartouches and other designs in shallow relief. Above the doorway, the virtuosity of the workmen is displayed in the balcony windows,

repeated on all four sides, which appear to be supported on a receding-bracket motif with overhanging banana buds. No surface is left unadorned, and there is throughout a subtle difference between deep, three-dimensional perforated carving and light, relief carving. The interior is equally innovative structurally and is elegantly conceived. The small mosque associated with this gate is less interesting; its minarets were demolished some time ago, only to be restored recently.

Following a road running southeast, visitors will reach the mosque of Ali Shahid Pir. This belonged to a compound that accommodated a rest house and saintly tomb, entered by a gate, now mostly vanished. Ali Shahid Pir was a contemporary of Ali I, the sultan who was probably responsible for this mosque, as suggested by cusped designs on the arches of its façade. The mosque's interior is of interest because of the vault running parallel to its façade. The *mihrab*, which is seven-sided, has a tall dome on intersecting arches that form kite-shaped pendentives. The door inside the *mihrab* may have permitted direct access to another building, but this has not survived. Another unusual interior feature is the panelled vaulting in the corners, a

Mihtar Mahal, famous for its excellent carved décor, c. 1620

The unfinished *Jami Masjid* begun by Ali I in 1574

Mihrab in *Jami Masjid*, 1636

motif recalling the Portuguese churches of Goa, as well as the chain with hanging ornament, a favourite Adil Shahi design. The *mihrab* was originally decorated with tiles, as was the Quranic inscription in white against a blue ground that ran above it. Recent restoration and repainting have sadly altered the character of this small but elegant example of early Adil Shahi religious architecture.

The nearby Asen Beg mosque is also called Yusuf's Old Jami, probably in reference to Yusuf Adil Khan. The inscription above the door frame records that this mosque was built during the reign of the Bahmani sultan Mahmud Shah, and that its cost was disbursed by Asen Beg Naib Ghaibat Adil Khani in the year 1512–13, when Yusuf Adil Khan's son Ismail Khan was governor of Bijapur.

Leaving these small mosques, visitors may continue eastwards to the *Jami Masjid*, located on the main thoroughfare linking the Allahpur Darwaza in the eastern sector of the city walls, with the southern gate to the citadel. The great congregational mosque of Bijapur was begun by Ali I in 1574, nine years after Talikota, but was never completed. A spectacular *mihrab*, by far the finest in the Deccan, was added by Muhammad Adil Shah in 1636; the gate on the eastern side of the courtyard is attributed to Aurangzeb after he occupied Bijapur. The grandly scaled mosque has a central pool, which once had a fountain fed with water conducted by earthen pipes from the Bari Baoli to the southeast of the mosque, close to Fath Darwaza. The original arched gateway to the mosque was from the north, where two-storeyed arcaded projections frame the main entrance, reached by steps. At the end of these projections are small square rooms with arched openings, each roofed with a dome framed by pinnacles at the four corners. They may have served as viewing platforms for the religious processions that took place along this major street of the city.

The prayer hall of the *Jami Masjid* comprises 45 spacious bays, defined by massive square columns that support lofty domes on kite-shaped pendentives. Its nine-bay arched façade is plastered, with a basalt parapet with arched niches. The *qibla* wall on either side of the *mihrab* displays arched niches, as did the walls of the wings on each side of the prayer hall where windows with diverse *jali* screens are now seen. On the eastern side of these wings are the polygonal bases of the mosque's unfinished basalt minarets. Their shafts are surrounded by lotus-petal designs and rest on the typical "footstool" motif found in most Adil Shahi monuments. The central dome of the *Jami Masjid* rests externally on a clerestory with arched niches and pinnacles; similar pinnacles would probably have decorated the façades. Internally, the dome occupies the nine central bays of the prayer hall. Designs with glazed tiles have been sparingly used on the surfaces that frame the arches, while the floor is covered in polished plaster. During the Mughal occupation, the floor was outlined in black to mark prayer spaces for devotees. The glory of the mosque's interior is, however, its deep, five-sided *mihrab* fashioned in high-quality basalt. This is possibly the work of the

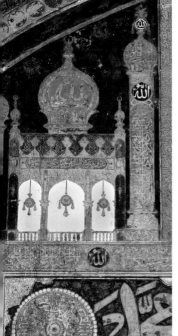

Detail of the delicately carved and painted basalt *mihrab* in the *Jami Masjid*, 1636

Habshi Yaqut Dabuli, who is mentioned in the inscriptions. The *mihrab* is delicately carved in low relief with inscriptions and ornamental motifs in tracery work, including foliate designs, hanging *alams*, brackets supporting roundels, images of buildings with bulbous domes, trompe l'œil illusionistic depictions of books recalling European themes, and vases inspired by Chinese originals. These are all painted on gesso plaster in blue, gold, red and magenta.

The elegant 17th-century Nau Gumbad, or Nine-Dome Mosque, stands a short distance northwest of the *Jami Masjid*. Its roof combines domes with pyramidal vaults, creating a pleasingly balanced stepped composition. Plaster designs adorn the arches of its main elevation, while on its southern wall steps lead to the roof. *Chhatris* mark the four corners of the mosque, and the main façade had two pinnacles. Although the interior has been damaged by numerous repaintings, the designs on the domes may still be seen, as can the Quranic inscriptions that run around the polished basalt *mihrab*. This building stands on land that once belonged to Khawass Khan, Prime Minister of Sikandar Shah, the last Adil Shahi sultan. The remains of his palace are located nearby, and it was here that Aurangzeb resided after conquering the city.

SHAHPUR AND AFZALPUR

Some 3 kilometres northwest of Bijapur's city walls, overlooking the valley of the Ramling river, is the suburb of Shahpur founded by Ali I to commemorate his enthronement in 1557. The subsequent growth of Shahpur, like that of Bijapur itself, followed the defeat of Vijayanagara at Talikota. Shahpur was developed as a great commercial centre, especially for textiles such as cotton muslins and calicoes that were transported to Dabhol and Chaul. At its height Shahpur's population rivalled that of Bijapur itself; this is reflected in the number and size of its monuments, even though these are now much dilapidated. The principal remains of Shahpur include the large and impressive Hauz-i-Shahpur, or reservoir and dam to the west together with an impressive water pavilion; and an impressive palace, or *sarai*, to the east. On a hillock to the south of the reservoir is the most venerated Sunni Chishti *dargah* in all of Bijapur. This was begun by Shah Miranji (d. 1499), continued by his son, Burhan al-Din Janam (d. 1597), and grandson, al-Din A'la (d. 1675), before being finally completed in 1677. Thus, while the Adil Shahi sultans tended to follow Shi'a Islam, and did not as a rule welcome Sunni Sufi figures, the hill at Shahpur kept Chishti Sufism alive. Visitors approach the summit of Shahpur hillock through an arched gate. In the middle of a large plaza full of tombstones rises the octagonal tomb of Amin al-Din A'la. The constant repairs and repaintings to which this tomb has been subjected over the years have partly obliterated its original stucco surface decoration. Around the monument are a number of interesting buildings, all associated with the *dargah*. A short distance to the north, along a wide north-south avenue on another hill, stands a long narrow *sarai* and a mosque. The impressive two-storeyed *sarai* has arcades on its northern and southern faces. Projecting brackets below the upper arches would have carried a

Chishti *dargah* in Shahpur, *c.* 1500

timber or stone balcony, perhaps to accommodate some ceremonial function. Another, similar balcony was located at rooftop level.

Sarai located on a hill in Shahpur, 1543–80

Visitors enter the *sarai* at Shahpur from the southern gate. This is adorned with a lobed arch, a motif associated particularly with Ali I. Framing this gate are stone carvings also decorated with lobed arches and open-flower motifs, one of which displays lions with their front paws resting on the arch's apex. Interconnecting chambers inside the *sarai* display an array of differently decorated domes originally covered in plaster, as was the building itself. On the northern face of the *sarai*, instead of balconies, the upper floor projects outwards to create a wide, long open space supported by the arcade below. It is possible that on the eastern section of the *sarai*, now hidden under rubble, are the remains of a *hammam* and beyond it an impressive *baoli*.

The Hauz-i-Shahpur reservoir was built on the Ramling river to provide Bijapur with water. The facings of the dam display different masonry techniques, suggesting numerous modifications dating back to the 13th century, as is evident from the large stones set in earth rather than mortar. With the foundation of Shahpur,

Remains of a water pavilion at Hauz-i-Shahpur, 1543–80

Arcaded domed interior in the *sarai*

work at the dam resumed, this time with smaller stones embedded in mortar. Receding steps can be seen along the slope of the dam. Next to these are the remains of a splendid triple-storeyed water pavilion set against the dam wall, with arches on all three of its visible sides. An octagonal pool at ground-floor level connected the open spaces of the reservoir during the dry months with the interior of this pavilion. The elegant array of different types of domes, many with the same decorative themes, as in the *sarai*, suggests that both edifices belong to Ali I's constructional endeavours. Contained in the section of the pavilion built into the thickness of the dam are the engineering works that facilitated the hydraulic systems that were essential to the storage and distribution of water to both Shahpur and Bijapur. A lock, two sluices, corridors and steps were combined with living quarters on the second and third levels, suggesting that when the reservoir was not full this pavilion could be used for pleasurable pursuits. The tiered lock was attached to a 45-metre-long culverted canal, which supplied water to the pools of a terraced garden to the east, which was probably added in the 17th century. Each level of the garden is marked by a narrow wall of arched niches, over which the water of the canal that joined all the pools would flow.

Northwest of the reservoir, near the road leading to Nauraspur (described below), is Takki or Afzalpur. This settlement takes its name from Afzal Khan, an able general under Muhammad and Ali II in the second half of the 17th century. Afzal Khan remains famous in Deccani history for capturing Shivaji's father, Shahji Bhonsle, who was at the time employed by the court of Bijapur, and imprisoning him for the misdeeds of his son who had been denounced as a rebel. Shivaji wanted to establish a Maratha kingdom, and his plunders and raids grew so irksome to the Adil Shahi rulers that they commissioned Afzal Khan to lead an expedition against him. Shivaji lured the Bijapur army to his mountainous stronghold of Pratapgad in western Maharashtra, where he treacherously murdered Afzal Khan in 1659. Although Afzal Kahn's tomb is located near Pratapgad, the construction of the Afzalpur tomb dated 1658–59 was probably completed by the general himself before embarking upon his last and fatal military expedition.

Tomb and mosque of Afzal Khan, Afzalpur, c. 1650

Pineapples
embellish the
central dome in
the tomb of Afzal
Khan, *c.* 1650

Afzal Khan's tomb and accompanying mosque, dated 1653, stand on a common platform surrounded by an arcade, with a small pool in between. Above the empty mausoleum, rises the dome supported on intersecting arches with corner recesses with benches, above which rise smaller domes on kite-shaped pendentives. The decoration of the central dome depicts *alams* and pineapples, a theme first recorded at the tomb of Afzal Khan's mentor, Muhammad Adil Shah. The mosque is unique in being a two-storeyed structure with *mihrabs* on both levels, but with a *minbar* only in the ground-floor hall. The *zenana* was on the upper floor, leaving the ground floor for the exclusive use of men, a scheme that may have been dictated by Afzal Khan's vast harem, most of whose occupants lie buried at a nearby bucolic location. This cemetery comprises eleven rows of tombs on a common platform built of plaster covered stone rubble. Their regular layouts might confirm the tale that Afzal Khan drowned his wives before leaving Bijapur to meet his death. The ruins of Afzal Khan's palace a short distance away suggest that this part of Shahpur may have formed part of his *jagir*, or territory, gifted by the state.

THE IBRAHIM RAUZA

A short distance beyond the Bijapur's walls, near the road running westwards from the Makka and Zohrapur Darwazas, is the

Ibrahim Rauza, the most beautiful and splendid of all Adil Shahi funerary monuments. According to the chronograms in poetic verses inscribed on the southern wall of the sepulchral chamber, Taj Sultana, Ibrahim's principal queen, offered this architectural masterpiece in 1633 to her husband, Ibrahim II, who had died seven years earlier in 1626. Both king and queen are buried in the austere and dark vaulted chamber of the mausoleum. After the queen's death, the work was completed by her trusted minister, the Habshi Malik Sandal.

Visitors enter the Ibrahim Rauza complex through an imposing gateway decorated with arched niches; its upper level is supported by ornamental brackets framed by two tall pinnacles with bulbous domes. A walled enclosure contains well-maintained lawns that surround on three sides the platform on which the tomb and its accompanying mosque are raised. Between the tomb and mosque, in the middle of the platform is a square pool with a fountain comprising an octagonal column topped by a lotus-flower spray. A stone awning originally covered two sides of the pool, shading those enjoying a cool moment here. In the northwest corner of the enclosure are the kitchens. The platform is supported on a colonnade, in which visitors, pilgrims and students could rest.

The juxtaposition of the stout, square bodies of matching tomb and mosque with their slightly bulbous domes springing from large lotus-petal friezes, surrounded by playful domed pinnacles of different heights and sizes, creates a splendid ensemble. The austere sepulchral chamber, surrounded by an arcade, is covered by a flat ceiling of stone slabs laid in mortar. Accompanied by members of their family are the nameless cenotaphs of Ibrahim II, his mother and Taj Sultana. The chamber is lit by arched window openings filled with exquisitely crafted, perforated-stone screens with Quranic inscriptions. The exterior walls of the sepulchral chamber, within the colonnaded verandah, display an array of carved and painted foliate themes combined with Arabic and Persian inscriptions. The teak doors are divided into panels with Arabic writing and decorative iron elements; they are framed by stone jambs incorporating complicated geometric patterns with possible magically protective properties. The verandah's ceiling is carved with additional foliate designs, including lotus medallions set in lobed cartouches. The arched reinforcements of the outer arcaded verandah are 19th-century restorations.

While the tomb at the Ibrahim Rauza is built entirely from beautifully carved basalt blocks, the mosque opposite combines plaster and stone. The *mihrab* within the domed prayer hall is deep and polygonal in plan and roofed with a tall dome. An even loftier dome roofs the central bay of the hall. Next to the *mihrab* is the *minbar*, originally surmounted by a miniature pavilion. This pavilion was later removed by Aurangzeb, and can now be seen in the Archaeological Museum at the Gol Gumbad.

Ibrahim's palace at Nauraspur, 1599

NAURASPUR

Located along the road running past the Ibrahim Rauza, 5 kilometres west of Bijapur, is Nauraspur, the twin city constructed in 1599 by Ibrahim II. Like Bijapur itself, Nauraspur was laid out as an approximate circle, but only the barest traces of its outer ramparts survive. Nauraspur takes its name from the Nauras cult, in which Ibrahim, as sultan and mystic, was both initiator and chief celebrant. The Nauras was a synthesis of the two most popular devotional cults in this part of Deccan: that of the Dattatreya saint Narasimha Sarasvati, and that of the Chishti Sufi saint Gesu Daraz. Historians record that 20,000 labourers were engaged in the construction of Nauraspur, while Bijapur's elite vied with each other to erect lavish residences. The now ruinous state of this royal foundation is a consequence of the 1624 war against the Nizam Shahi kingdom of Ahmadnagar, the army of which was led by the Habshi Malik Ambar. The walls of Naurasur had not yet been completed when Ibrahim took refuge in Bijapur, leaving his city to the mercy of Malik Ambar's troops. Disheartened, Ibrahim never returned to his new city.

Nauraspur comprises three adjoining walled enclosures. The largest and most impressive is a vast walled compound with pointed arched openings in each of the nine sides, with Ibrahim's palace at the centre. Only the stone skeleton of this palace survives; the interior, probably in timber, was destroyed during the Nizam Shahi attack. Like the great audience halls in the citadel of Bijapur, Nauraspur also has a great masonry arch flanked by smaller ones facing north towards a courtyard with a pool. To the north of this enclosure was the *zenana*, with another royal edifice and *hammam*, now in a dilapidated state. To the south are the remains of what may have been the administrative centre of the palace and, at one time, the entire kingdom.

Nauraspur was built next to the Torweh reservoir, but was also supplied with water from the Surang Baoli. This was channelled under the city walls of Bijapur through a great subterranean tunnel that ran from the Makka Darwaza, via the Taj Baoli in the western part of Bijapur, to Nauraspur. The twin city was also once connected to Bijapur via a large commercial avenue, of which nothing now survives.

The palace of Jahan Begum at Ainapur, c. 1650

AINAPUR

The suburb of Ainapur, 3 kilometres beyond Bijapur's railway station to the east of the city walls, was known in the 17th century as Jahanama, after its founder Jahan Begum, the wife of Muhammad Adil Shah. The ruins of the small but elegantly proportioned garden palace built by Jahan Begum in her landed estate at Ainapur

The unfinished tomb of Jahan Begum, which was intended as a copy of her husband's mausoleum, the Gol Gumbad, c. 1660

are now located in open fields. On the western and eastern sides of the palace, two *baolis* provided water for the surrounding lands. Recently, the tomb of a saint has been established under the banyan tree near a pool in front of the dilapidated arcaded palace façade. Behind this façade is a raised vestibule with octagonal plastered stone columns, capitals and brackets, the only intact examples of these features in any Adil Shahi palace. This vestibule is framed by long rectangular rooms; to the south is a reception hall with an elevated sitting area that is treated as a throne, with a small dome carried on pendentives. Steps from here lead to the upper levels and roof terrace of the palace.

The unfinished tomb of Jahan Begum, a short distance from the palace, was evidently intended as a copy of her husband's mausoleum, the great Gol Gumbad, replicating its exact form and dimensions. However, the façades of the queen's tomb were never completed, and only the four corner towers survive. Between these are two intermediate, lesser towers with arched niches to support a monumental central arch and two smaller side arches that were never built. These tripartite compositions are repeated on the interior of the sepulchral chamber, to frame the raised platform where the beautifully carved cenotaph of the queen can still be seen, beside four smaller cenotaphs. The actual burials are located in the vaulted chamber below, accessed from a northern entrance.

Restored water pavilions in Kumatgi, 17th century

Water pavilions and a hydraulic device

The tomb is surrounded on three sides by circular pools, with a small mosque to the west within the walled compound.

KUMATGI

The royal resort at Kumatgi, 12 kilometres east of Bijapur, dates from the 17th century, most likely towards the end of Ibrahim II's reign. Kumatgi was an elite recreational site and also a commercial centre since it was located on the principal route linking Bijapur with its eastern provinces. The resort occupies a verdant valley with numerous pleasure pavilions whose water features were fed by a great lake with a dam and a complex system of hydraulic works. The buildings most visited today stand in a fenced enclosure beneath the western face of the dam wall. The first pavilion to be seen here is a rectangular building with a five-arched façade. Its interior, with octagonal and lotus-shaped pools set into the floor, is divided into five bays by transverse arches, each bay roofed with a small dome carried on interlocking kite-shaped pendentives. Badly damaged murals depicting courtly and recreational activities are comparable to those in the Asar Mahal near the citadel. Some of the better-preserved compositions depict a sultan in discussion with a Sufi, a mounted rider, and an array of beautiful flowering plants. The other pavilion at Kumatgi is a two-storeyed square structure topped by an onion-shaped dome that functioned as a storage tank from which water was sprayed through copper shower-roses into the chamber that occupied the pavilion's upper level. The outer walls of the room at the lower level are surrounded by stone spouts fashioned as geese from which water gushed into the surrounding basin.

Immediately outside the enclosure is a lofty but ruined masonry tower. This probably accommodated a series of vertically interlocking wooden wheels with small buckets that lifted water from the dam to an elevated cistern, all now lost. This would have been an effective method of achieving the required pressure to work the fountains in the nearby pavilions.

Visitors are encouraged to walk along the top of the dam wall beside the lake from where they may enjoy a sunset view from a domed chamber that projects over the water. However, a boat will be required to reach the small island pavilion that can be seen in the middle of the water. Additional features at Kumatgi, such as a dilapidated arched gate leading to a large avenue and several other pavilions, can be seen in the fields to the west of the enclosure.

ACKNOWLEDGEMENTS

I would like to thank for their support and advice George Michell, Pushkar Sohoni and Tony Korner. Klaus Rotzer for his help these last few years. Ameen Hullur for his help while in Bijapur. Surendra Kumar for his lovely panoramic photographs.

The British Library London has kindly permitted the publication of Colin Mackenzie's water colours.

GLOSSARY

Afaqi foreigner

alam Shia commemorative standard

al-asma al-husna the Beautiful Names of God

al-ikhlas Purity of (Faith); Sura CXII of the Quran

al-kahf the Cave; Sura XVIII of the Quran

baoli step-well

baraka blessing, prosperity

bhakti Hindu devotional sects; loving devotion to a deity

chhajja stone awning

chhatri small-domed, open-pillared kiosk

Chishti devotee linked to the most popular South-Asian Sufi sect

Dakhini Deccani

dargah "court" (usually of a saint); Sufi convent, hospice, dwelling or tomb

darshan sight; "vision of the divine"

darwaza gate

Diwan-i-Am public audience hall

dolerite a fine basalt stone of deep green colour

guldasta "bunch of flowers"; fluted pinnacle

Habshi sub-Saharan Africans; the Arabic word for Abyssinian or Ethiopian

hammam Turkish variant of a steam bath

hauz pool; tank

hazar sutun thousand-columned hall

idgah open-air prayer platform with wall facing Mecca

iwan arched vaulted hall enclosed on three sides and open on one

jagir territory given to a grandee of the state.

jali stone-carved openwork screen with designs

jama'at khana gathering hall

jami congregational, Friday mosque

kalima Muslim confession of faith

khalifa one who receives the khilafat; designated successor of Prophet or saint

Kufic Arabic script distinguished by geometric shapes

lotus-tree motif design found in Bahmani royal, Sufi and elite tombs, consisting of a triangular leaf shape standing on a trunk and filled with lotus scrolls or inscriptions

madrasa school for traditional Islamic sciences

mandala sacred geometric diagram of the structure of the universe

mandapa columned hall preceding a sanctuary in a Hindu or Jain temple

masha'ikh generic term for saints or religious elders

masjid mosque

mihrab prayer niche on a mosque's qibla wall

minbar pulpit in a mosque

muluk khana royal enclosure in a mosque

muqarnas "stalactite" or "honeycomb" ornaments or vaulting comprising concave elements; geometric compositions

murid disciple of a pir

naqqar khanna drum house, or the place where musicians performed during ceremonies or special hours of the day

pir spiritual leader; Sufi master

pishtaq portal associated with an iwan

qanat well-like vertical shafts connected by sloping tunnels that tap into subterranean water

qibla direction of prayer: towards Mecca

sarai palace or station for travellers and merchants

shahada confession of faith

urs wedding or death anniversary of a pir

Wali custodian, protector, friend of God, saint

zenana part of a house reserved for women

DYNASTIC LISTS

Bahmanis of Gulbarga And Bidar

Alauddin Hasan Gangu Bahman Shah	1347–1358
Muhammad Shah I	1358–1375
Mujahid Shah	1375–1378
Dawud Shah I	1378
Muhammad Shah II	1378–1397
Ghiyathuddin	1397
Shamsuddin	1397
Tajuddin Firuz Shah	1397–1422
Ahmad Shah Wali I	1422–1436
Alauddin Ahmad Shah II	1436–1458
Humayun Shah	1458–1461
Nizamuddin Ahmad Shah III	1461–1463
Muhammad Shah III	1463–1482
Mahmud Shah	1482–1518
Ahmad Shah IV	1518–1521
Allaudin Shah	1521–1522
Walilullah	1522–1525
Kalimullah	1525–1527

Baridis of Bidar

Qasim I	–1504
Amir I	1504–1543
Ali Shah	1543–1580
Ibrahim	1580–1587
Qasim II	1587–1591
Amir II	1591–1600
Mirza	1600–1609
Amir III	1609–1619

Adil Shahis of Bijapur

Yusuf Adil Khan	1490–1510
Ismail Adil Khan	1510–1534
Mallu Adil Khan	1534–1535
Ibrahim I	1535–1558
Ali I	1558–1580
Ibrahim II	1580–1627
Muhammad	1627–1656
Ali II	1656–1672
Sikandar	1672–1686

SELECT BIBLIOGRAPHY

Ali, Daud and Emma Flatt, eds. *Garden and Landscape Practices in Pre-colonial India: Histories from the Deccan*, Delhi, 2011.

Cousens, Henry, *Bijapur and its Architectural Remains with an Historical Outline of the Adil Shahi Dynasty*, New Delhi, 1996.

Eaton, R.M., *Sufis of Bijapur 1300–1700, Social Roles of Sufis in Medieval India*, Princeton, 1978 and New Delhi, 1996.

----, *The New Cambridge History of India I, 8: A Social History of the Deccan, 1300–1761, Eight Indian Lives*, Cambridge, 2005.

Ernst, C.W., *Eternal Garden, Mysticism, History, and Politics at a South Asian Sufi Center*, Albany, NY, 1992.

Hegewald, Julia A.B., *Water Architecture in South Asia, A Study of Types, Developments and Meanings*, Leiden, 2002.

Haidar, Navina Najat and Marika Sardar, eds., *Sultans of the South: Arts of India's Deccan Courts, 1323–1687*, Metropolitan Museum, New York, 2011.

Hutton, Deborah, *Art of the Court of Bijapur*, Bloomington and Indianapolis, 2006.

Imaratwale, Abdul Gani, *History of Bijapur Subah (1686–1885)*, New Delhi, 2007.

Khalidi, Omar, Dakan *Under the Sultans, 1296–1724, A Bibliography of Monographic and Periodical Literature*, Wichita, Kansas, 1987.

Merklinger, Elizabeth, Seven Tombs at Holkonda: A Preliminary Survey, *Kunst des Orients*, X 1/2: 187-97, 1975.

-----, *Indian Islamic Architecture: The Deccan 1347–1686*, Warminster, 1981.

-----, *Sultanate Architecture of Pre-Mughal India*, Delhi, 2005.

Michell, George, ed., *Islamic Heritage of the Deccan*, Bombay, 1986.

Michell, George and Richard Eaton, *Firuzabad, Palace City of the Deccan*, Oxford, 1992.

Michell George and Mark Zebrowski, *The New Cambridge History of India I.7, Architecture and Art of the Deccan Sultanates*, Cambridge, 1999.

Nayeem, N.A., *The Heritage of the Adil Shahis of Bijapur,* Hyderabad, 2008.

Philon, Helen, The murals in the tomb of Ahmad Shah near Bidar, *Apollo*, CLII, no. 465, pp. 3-10, 2000.

----- ed., *Silent Splendour: Palaces of the Deccan, 14th–19th Centuries*, Mumbai, 2010.

Rotzer, Klaus, Bijapur: Alimentation en eau d'une ville Musulmane du Dekkan aux XVIe-XVIIe siècles, *Bulletin de l'Ecole Français d'Extrême-Orient*, LXXIII: 125-95, 1984.

Sherwani, H.K., *The Bahmanis of the Deccan*, New Delhi, 1985.

Sherwani, H.K. and P.M. Joshi, eds., *History of Medieval Deccan (1295–1724)*, Hyderabad, 2 vols., 1973–74.

Siddiqui, M.S., *The Bahmani Sufis*, Delhi, 1989.

Yazdani, G., *Bidar, Its History and Monuments*, New Delhi, 1995.

Zebrowski, Mark, *Deccani Painting*, London, 1983.

INDEX